yalsa
Young Adult Library
Services Association
a division of the
American Library Association

Teens
at the **Library**
SERIES

Evaluating Teen Services and Programs

D0556804

Sarah Flowers

Neal-Schuman
An imprint of the American Library Association
Chicago 2012

Published in cooperation with the Young Adult Library Services Association.

Printed in the United States of America
16 15 14 13 12   5 4 3 2 1

Extensive effort has gone into ensuring the reliability of the information in this book; however, the publisher makes no warranty, express or implied, with respect to the material contained herein.

ISBNs: 978-1-55570-793-4 (paper); 978-1-55570-851-1 (PDF)

Library of Congress Cataloging-in-Publication Data
Flowers, Sarah, 1952–
    Evaluating teen services and programs : a YALSA guide / Sarah Flowers.
        p. cm.
    Includes bibliographical references and index.
    ISBN 978-1-55570-793-4
    1. Young adults' libraries—Evaluation—United States. 2. Libraries and teenagers—United States. I. Young Adult Library Services Association. II. Title.

Z718.5.F58 2012
027.62'6—dc23
                                                                            2012015105

Cover design by Rosemary Holderby, Cole Design & Production
Text design in Bodoni and Univers Condensed by UB Communications

♾ This paper meets the requirements of ANSI/NISO Z39.48-1992 (Permanence of Paper).

Contents

List of Illustrations

Figures

Tables

Forms

Foreword

In tough economic times, funders want to know the value of what they are funding, and not just the monetary value, but how the library is making a difference in the community and in the lives of patrons. Administrators want to know how budget dollars are being spent to improve teen services, and you want to know if the programs and services you are developing and implementing for and with teens at your library are effective. To gather the information you need to answer all of these questions, you must first develop a plan for evaluating your comprehensive teen program. Lucky for you, past YALSA President and teen program evaluation guru Sarah Flowers has developed *Evaluating Teen Services and Programs* to be your step-by-step guide in this process, from data collection to analysis.

I had the good fortune of serving on the YALSA Board of Directors with author Sarah Flowers, and from working closely with her over the years, I know that Sarah has not only a passion for serving teens but also the experience and knowledge necessary to help educate professionals who are new to teen services. While Sarah and I served together on the YALSA Board, she headed up a task force whose mission was to develop the YALSA Public Library Evaluation Tool. After reading through the evaluation tool and actually using it to evaluate Charlotte Mecklenburg Library's comprehensive teen program, I knew that what we needed was to go one step further and provide library staff with directions for drafting goals and objectives; gathering, measuring, and analyzing data; creating a community needs assessment; and developing a strategic plan. *Evaluating Teen Services and Programs* is the comprehensive guide I had hoped for, filled with the background knowledge and ready-to-use evaluation forms and checklists you need to assess your library's current teen program, support your case for improved teen services, and evaluate your library's overall level of success in providing library services to teens.

Michele Gorman
Author, *Connecting Young Adults and Libraries: A How-To-Do-It Manual*
Teen Services Coordinator, Charlotte Mecklenburg Library
Editor, Teens at the Library Series

Preface

Today's generation of teens is the largest and most diverse ever. Keeter and Taylor (2009), writing for the Pew Research Center, report that among Millennials, today's teens and twenty-somethings, "18.5 percent are Hispanic; 14.2 percent are black; 4.3 percent are Asian; 3.2 percent are mixed race or other; and 59.8 percent, a record low, are white." According to a survey conducted in 2007 by Harris Interactive for the American Library Association (ALA, 2007), 78 percent of youth aged 8–18 reported having a public library card. Eighty-one percent of those reported visiting the public or school library during the past year.

Are you prepared to serve these young people when they show up at your library? The good news is that libraries are stepping up to the challenge of serving teens appropriately. We know this from two surveys taken thirteen years apart. In 1994, a survey by the National Center for Education Statistics (NCES) indicated that, despite the fact that teens comprised 25 percent of library users, only 11 percent of U.S. libraries had at least one staff person dedicated to serving teens. By 2007, when the Public Library Data Service (PLDS) poll questioned libraries about teens, 62 percent of libraries surveyed indicated that they have at least one staff person serving teens. Similarly, the PLDS survey showed that about 84 percent of main libraries and 72 percent of branches housed young adult (YA) materials in a separate area from children's or adult materials, up from 58 percent in 1994 (Mustafoff and Teffeau, 2008).

Having a staff member dedicated to serving teens and having a separate teen collection are excellent starting places, but those things alone do not mean that the library's teen programs and services are the best that they can be. In *Evaluating Teen Services and Programs: A YALSA Guide*, I explore some ways that anyone can go about evaluating the teen programs and services in a library and start the process of improving those services. The primary audiences for this book include teen services librarians, library generalists, youth or adult services librarians who have been tasked with serving teens, library directors, library school students studying teen services, and middle school and high school librarians. I do not assume that the reader has a strong background in teen services, in methods of data gathering, or in models of evaluation. This truly is a primer that covers the basics of what you need to know to begin evaluating your library's programs and services.

During my career as a manager and administrator at a major public library system, I have observed that many librarians are uneasy around numbers, statistics, graphs, and charts. And yet gathering and analyzing these types of data can be critical to your overall success. Data can point you to the places you need to make changes. If, for example, circulation of teen materials is 20 percent of the library's circulation, but teen materials get only 2 percent of the library's materials budget, you may be able to make a case for a budget increase in this area. If teens make up 30 percent of your service area, but are responsible for only 5 percent of circulation, you may need to look at ways to build a collection or services that will have a greater appeal to this age group, or at ways to take the collection to the teens. There are many other kinds of data as well, both objective and subjective, that will help you make outstanding teen services part of the whole library experience, every day.

In addition to my work experience in using data to analyze library programs and services, for the past several years I have worked with other YALSA members to update and revise YALSA's Competencies for Librarians Serving Youth, and to create a Teen Services Evaluation Tool. These experiences, as well as my experience in writing a book about the competencies for YALSA, have convinced me that libraries are hungry for practical information about how to improve their teen programs and services. In *Evaluating Teen Services and Programs: A YALSA Guide*, I hope to demystify the process of collecting and analyzing data, and show how it can lead to meaningful evaluation of library programs and services.

Chapter 1 looks at who teens are, the reasons why we serve teens in libraries, and where libraries fit into their basic developmental needs. In addition, the chapter shows how evaluating teen programs and services will help you make them a better fit for the specific teens in your community and where teen programs and services fit into the whole library experience. Chapter 2 focuses on the planning stages of evaluation. It begins with a look at how to develop effective goals and objectives for evaluating your programs, because you can't just begin an evaluation without some idea of where you've been and where you're headed. Then the chapter goes on to explain some of the types of data you will want to collect, as well as where to find the data. Chapter 3 moves into the implementation phase, beginning with analyzing the data you have collected and exploring ways to use the data to make changes and plan for the future. Chapter 4 focuses on evaluating specific programs: teen collections, teen summer reading programs, ongoing teen programs and special events, and library staff. Chapter 5 looks at some best practices in evaluating programs and services, focusing on YALSA's Competencies and the Teen Services Evaluation Tool. Chapter 6 contains references and resources to help you with evaluating your programs, including sample forms and checklists. Throughout the book, I include real-life examples to illustrate the types of data collection, data analysis, and evaluation rubrics you can use in examining your own programs and services.

I hope you'll find that *Evaluating Teen Services and Programs: A YALSA Guide* helps you to analyze and evaluate your library's teens services, with the ultimate goal of providing excellent library service for and with teens.

References

ALA (American Library Association). 2007. "American Library Association Youth and Library Use Study." American Library Association. http://www.ala.org/yalsa/sites/ala.org.yalsa/files/content/professionaltools/HarrisYouthPoll.pdf.

Keeter, Scott, and Paul Taylor. 2009. "The Millennials." Pew Research Center, December 11. http://www.pewresearch.org/pubs/1437/millennials-profile.

Mustafoff, Megan, and Lauren Teffeau. 2008. "Young Adult Services and Technology in Public Libraries: An Analysis of the 2007 Public Library Data Service." *Public Libraries* 47, no. 1: 12–13.

Acknowledgments

I would like to thank my colleagues at YALSA, who continue to inspire me with their dedication to serving teens in the best possible way. It is an honor to work with you. Thanks also to Michele Gorman, the series editor for this book, who approached me about writing this book and encouraged me along the way. I would also like to thank the Santa Clara County Library in California, where I learned on the job many of the techniques used in the book. I especially appreciate the assistance of Nancy Howe, Derek Wolfgram, and Peggy Tomasso in providing me with statistics and reports that I could use in creating many of the examples in this book. Thanks also to Mark Flowers, Solano County (CA) Library; Penny Johnson, Baraboo (WI) Public Library; and Stephanie Squicciarini, Fairport (NY) Public Library for sharing their statistics and forms with me. Finally, thanks to my family for supporting me always.

1

Background and Theory

Adolescent Development

Teens are developmentally different from children and from adults, and those differences affect the ways library workers interact with teens in the library. It is important to start with a basic understanding of who teens are and the developmental tasks they face, because those factors affect everything else, from the specific programs and services libraries offer to the ways that library staff members provide assistance to the teen who is standing in front of them at a service desk. Knowing something about adolescent development can help library workers provide a positive library experience for teens—and that, in turn, is a great way to help teens grow and, at the same time, to create a healthier and better integrated community.

Adolescence can be a turbulent time for teens and for those around them. One look can tell you that a teenager is no longer a cute little kid, but just because he may look like an adult doesn't mean he's there yet. Teens still have a lot of growing to do, sometimes physically, but always emotionally, socially, and psychologically. One challenge is that teenagers can act like adults one minute and like children the next. It is sometimes hard to know what to expect, which is why many adults are wary around teens. People often refer to the turbulence of adolescence as being due to "hormones," and it's true that testosterone and estrogen are making themselves felt in all sorts of ways. But in the past ten years or so, scientists have been learning a lot about the teenage brain. "Using powerful new brain-scanning machines, peering for the first time into living, working teenage brains . . . neuroscientists are finding that the teenage brain, far from being an innocent bystander to hormonal hijinks, is undergoing a dramatic transformation" (Strauch, 2003: 7–8).

We used to think that because brains reach adult size early in adolescence, they stopped developing then as well. In recent years, however, scientists have discovered that the teen brain is still growing and developing at a rapid pace. "Adolescent brains 'are only about 80 percent of the way to maturity,' [Dr. Frances Jenson, a neuroscientist at Harvard] said at the annual meeting of the Society for Neuroscience in November [2010]. It takes until the mid-20s, and possibly later, for a brain to become fully developed" (Juskalian, 2010). The corpus callosum, the "thick cable of nerves that connects the two halves of the brain and is involved in creativity and higher type of thinking," doesn't reach full maturity until humans are in their twenties (Giedd, 2002). The parietal lobes, which integrate auditory, visual, and tactile signals, remain immature until about age 16, and the temporal lobes, which are linked to both language and emotional maturity, are still developing after 16. The frontal lobe, specifically the prefrontal cortex, is the part of the brain involved in impulse control, judgment, and emotional regulation. This area is completely restructured during the teen years, which helps to explain why teens are prone to emotional outbursts and risk-taking behaviors.

What is particularly interesting for adults who work with teens in libraries and elsewhere is the fact that the activities teens participate in can be a factor in how their brains will develop. According to research done by Dr. Jay Giedd of the National Institutes of Mental Health (NIMH), teens "who 'exercise' their brains by learning to order their thoughts, understand abstract concepts, and control their impulses are laying the neural foundations that will serve them for the rest of their lives. 'This argues for doing a lot of things as a teenager,' says Dr. Giedd. 'You are hard-wiring your brain in adolescence. Do you want to hard-wire it for sports and playing music and doing mathematics—or for lying on the couch in front of the television?'" (ACT for Youth Center of Excellence, 2002: 1).

The psychologist Erik Erikson said that the main question of adolescence is "Who am I and where am I going?" (*Wikipedia*, 2012). That sums up a lot of what teens are going through. Probably the most important task of the adolescent is the movement toward independence. At around 12 or 13, teens become capable of abstract thinking, moving out of the concrete thinking that is typical of younger children. This is when they can learn algebra and start to notice symbolism in literature. They can hypothesize, think about the future, and foresee the consequences of their actions. Their ability to use speech and writing to express themselves blossoms.

This abstract thinking helps them move toward becoming individuals, entirely separate from their parents. It may seem at this point that teens are rejecting their parents and other adults but, in fact, they are learning how to love and respect adults without being totally dependent on them. They are learning how to relate *as* adults to other adults. They are also making decisions about what life will look like for them in the future: What kind of career or vocation will they have? How will they achieve that? What will their family life be like? Will they marry? Have children? Are they attracted to same-sex or opposite-sex partners? How will they participate in society at large? What are their moral values—not just what have they been told, but what do they really believe? Teens are also learning to accept their own physical bodies. Because their bodies are going through major changes at this time, they are often very self-conscious about them. Because some of these ways of thinking are new, they are also often self-conscious about them as well.

Millennials

Today's teens are part of a larger group known as Millennials (those born between 1981 and 2000). They are a large and diverse group, and among the most ethnically and racially diverse in U.S. history. Millennials are, as the Pew Research Center says, "the first generation in human history who regard behaviors like tweeting and texting, along with websites like Facebook, YouTube, Google and Wikipedia, not as astonishing innovations of the digital era, but as everyday parts of their social lives and their search for understanding" (Pew Research Center, 2010). They are actually more inclined to trust in institutions than either Baby Boomers or Gen Xers (those who are now 30–45 years old).

In the fall of 2009, Lee Rainie of the Pew Internet & American Life Project gave a presentation on "Teens in the Digital Age." In it, he draws some conclusions about how the digital age has affected the learning styles of today's teens, who are what he calls "networked learners." These young people are, he says:

- More self-directed and less dependent on top-down instructions
- Better arrayed to capture new information inputs
- More reliant on feedback and response
- More attuned to group outreach and group knowledge
- More open to cross-discipline insights, creating their own "tagged" taxonomies
- More oriented toward people being their own individual nodes of production (Rainie, 2009: 22)

Thinking about these characteristics in terms of library use, it is easy to see why many teens, unlike older populations, may prefer to work in group study rooms, rather than at isolated study carrels, and why they have a different approach to using tools such as the library catalog.

Serving Diverse Teens

But again, these are all generalizations, and not a description of the teen who is standing in front of you in the library. For one thing, 12-year-olds and 18-year-olds often have very different interests, as may boys and girls. Some teens are avid readers, some still struggle with reading, and others can read, but just prefer not to (or at least not to read books). Teens don't all like the same kind of music—their tastes vary as widely as those of adults—and they can be very knowledgeable about the kind of music they do like, whether it's classical, hip-hop, classic rock, country, ska, emo, or some genre you have never heard of. Teens, like adults, are from different ethnic backgrounds, different religious backgrounds, and different socioeconomic backgrounds. Knowing the demographics of your community is useful, but it is never a good idea to assume that the teen in front of you fits into any sort of niche. No one likes to be labeled, and teens are no exception. But knowing something about the ethnic, cultural, and religious groups in your community may help you understand the needs and attitudes of your library's users, especially if they differ from your own.

In a paper written for YALSA in 2011, Queens College Professor and young adult library services pioneer Mary K. Chelton noted: "By 2020, the projected number of people over 65 will equal those people under 18." She continued:

> These demographic realities beg for culturally competent service and culturally authentic materials, the political will to advocate for young people in the face of hostility or indifference on the part of the senior population, which is starting to include the retiring baby boomers, and a strong push for intergenerational alliances. Making old people know and love teenagers should become an overt and covert goal of all YA services providers in the decade ahead, or generational competition for resources, predictably exploited by politicians and the media, will effectively kill or starve services for adolescents across the board at all levels of government. (Chelton, 2011: 4–5)

Teens interact with the library in many different ways. Some teens simply want a comfortable chair in which to read, all the while keeping their eye on what is going on around them. Other teens primarily want to hang out with friends. Some teens want to use the computers, or game consoles, or board games. Others need service hours for school, and want to volunteer. And, of course, many teens need to use the library to find information.

Information-Seeking Behavior

Teens who approach library staff generally do so with two main sorts of queries. The most common is the "imposed query," which is usually a school assignment. The other common type of question is the personal query, which is frequently a popular culture query (e.g., information about the hottest new singer,) or a query regarding their own life (drugs, sexuality, parental divorce, or just a desire for something good to read).

These kinds of queries can and do cause problems for library workers. Staff may dislike imposed queries because teens don't really seem that invested in the answer, or don't even know what the real question is. There can be a sense that helping with these queries is somehow unfair, and that library staff shouldn't be "doing their homework for them." Personal queries can seem to library staff to be problematic in a different way. If they involve popular culture topics, library staff may not even have heard of the topic yet. A fear of looking foolish or a sense that all such topics are ephemeral and unimportant can cause staff to dismiss these queries without making much effort. To complicate matters, many of the formal information sources that library staff are accustomed to using may not have much information on these topics.

Other kinds of personal queries may deal with issues that teens are reluctant to discuss out loud, such as sexuality or drugs. Still others may be easier for library staff to deal with, such as career or college information or information about hobbies or sports.

Library staff should be trained to understand that for the most part, working with teens is no different from working with any other library user. Good customer service skills are the key. Just like adults, teens want answers—correct answers—to the questions they bring to the library staff. They want to be treated with respect, they want to feel good about the transaction, and they want to learn something so they can be more independent in the future. While an adult may make the effort to "interrupt" a staff member who appears to be either busy or disengaged, teens often lack the self-confidence to approach such a person, so it is critical that library staff appear inviting and approachable. Teens often feel stupid asking for help because it increases the self-consciousness that is already present, so it is the job of library staff to make it clear that there is nothing we want more than to answer their questions. Approaching teens with a question like "Are you finding everything you need?" or "Hi, how can I help?" gives them the opportunity to ask for help without losing face.

Like many adult library users, teens will often begin by asking the question they think the library can answer, rather than the question they really have. This goes for both the questions they ask library staff and the queries they enter into the library catalog or web search engine. So they will ask if the library has "any books about war" when their assignment is to write an essay on the causes of World War I. Or they will enter the search term "World War I" into Google, and either become alarmed at the vast amount of information that shows up or simply take the first hit, which is probably a *Wikipedia* article, and fail to go any further.

In other ways, teens have a different approach to information gathering than many adults. Many library staff tend to assume that information is best acquired through what are known as formal information systems: catalogs, directories, books, formally organized websites, and so on. Teens (and many adults), on the other hand, tend to prefer informal information systems, in which they don't so much search for information as share it. This tendency has only been heightened by the use of the Internet and social networking. And, in fact, social sharing sites are often the best places to answer the personal or popular culture queries that teens have. Also, teens have grown up doing "group work" in school, and many of them prefer to do their library work that way as well. They will have their friends around them at the computer as they search for information and use feedback from the friends to help them find the answers.

Developmental Assets

Beginning in 1989, the Search Institute conducted surveys of sixth- through twelfth-graders in public and private schools all over the United States. In 1990, they first published their list of 40 Developmental Assets® for adolescents, which they defined as "40 common sense, positive experiences and qualities that help influence choices young people make and help them become caring, responsible adults." Their studies have shown that the more assets young people have, the more likely they are to thrive and the less likely to engage in high-risk behaviors (Search Institute, 2006).

In the 20 years since the assets were first defined, youth-serving professionals of all types, including library workers, have used them as a basis for planning and defending programs for teens. The library can provide some of the "external" assets, in the areas of support, empowerment, boundaries and expectations, and constructive use of time. These in turn allow teens to develop the "internal" assets, in the areas of commitment to learning, positive values (honesty, integrity, social justice), social competencies (conflict resolution, planning, and decision making), and positive identity.

This role of the library in helping teens develop assets fits neatly with the brain research discussed earlier. Since teens are developing neural pathways, those who work with teens can help the process by offering opportunities for them to "exercise" their brains. What's more, the success of programs and services can depend on whether developmental assets are taken into account in the planning process.

Youth Participation

One of the best ways to develop positive relationships with teens in the library is to involve them. Providing teens with opportunities to be active participants in library decision making empowers teens, gives them an opportunity to form relationships with adult library workers and with one another, and gives them constructive ways to use their time and opportunities to demonstrate—and expand—their own skills, all of which are important assets for teens.

Some libraries have formal teen advisory boards. These may come in many different forms, but their main purpose is to involve teens in responsible action and significant decision making in their library. A good teen advisory board will have adult guidance and support, but will not be dominated by adults. Teens will have the opportunity to provide input into library programs and materials and to participate in decisions on matters that affect them. Libraries that use teen advisory boards often find, for example, that their teen programs have better attendance because the teen advisors not only suggest programs of interest to themselves but also encourage their friends and peers to attend.

Some libraries have active teen volunteer programs, either instead of or in addition to an advisory board. Many high schools today require service learning hours, and volunteering at the library may be one way to meet that requirement. Other libraries utilize the expertise of the teens who are employed there as pages or shelvers, and still others take advantage of the existence of a local youth board that advises the city council or other governing body. The point to remember is that everything a library does for and with teens—collections, programs, facilities, services—can benefit from teen input. Not only do these types of opportunities give teens valuable experience and validation, they serve to introduce the rest of the library staff and members of the community to teens who are working positively to make the world a better place. Many teens who start as volunteers or members of teen advisory boards go on to become library workers themselves, and all of them have the potential to be great ambassadors for the library in the wider world.

The Whole Library Experience

To be truly effective, teen programs and services must fit into the whole library experience. Ideally, everyone in the library, from the top administrators to the volunteers, should understand that teen programs and services are part of what makes the library a real asset for the community. Teens are part of every community, and while some of their needs may be different from those of children and adults, they are still users of the library and deserving of equally respectful treatment.

The teens in one community may be very different from the teens in another, however. Teens are not a homogenous group, any more than adults are. The teens in any community will reflect the diversity of the community: ethnically, socially, economically, educationally, and in terms of religion, class, and interests. There is no one-size-fits-all version of teen library service, any more than there is a one-size-fits-all version of overall library service.

One of the interesting things about teens is that, unlike most children, who stay in the children's room, and most adults, who never venture out of the adult department, they often freely use the entire library for both recreational and informational needs. But because their learning styles and needs differ from those of adults and children, often library workers aren't quite sure how to deal with teens. It is simply not possible to relegate teen services to staff who are designated as "teen services librarians." The whole library's staff needs to have some understanding of who teens are and how they interact with the library. In the words of Linda W. Braun (2010), who wrote an issue paper for YALSA on the importance of a whole-library approach to teen services:

> A library with a strong commitment to young adults guarantees that the age group is treated with respect by the entire library staff. This is possible only when all staff take part in training related to the developmental assets of teens. Knowledge of these assets, and of why they are important to the successful growth of adolescents, provides library staff with a foundation from which to work when developing policies, collections and programs. This knowledge also provides an understanding of why teens behave as they do when inside a library as well as a comprehension of how to react to sometimes challenging young adult behaviors.

The integration of young adult services into the whole library experience extends to collection development. For both school assignments and personal needs, teens can find useful materials in both the children's and adult sections of the library as well as in areas specifically designated for young adults. Often the introduction to a new subject is best achieved by looking at a children's book, while only a book for adults will contain the level of detail that a teen wants or needs on another subject. As Braun (2010) notes:

> Young adult services staff, reference staff and children's services staff must work together to plan for collections that not only support the homework help needs of young adults, but also meet the personal information needs of the age group. Both male and female adolescents require opportunities to access materials such as those that support their personal interests from learning about relationships, to discovering options for life after high school, to finding out about current trends in entertainment or fashion. A full complement of materials such as magazines and books in the adult, teen, and children's areas of the library are required in order to support the educational, recreational and personal growth needs of teens at all levels of development.

Having a strong shared view of what excellent library service to teens should look like is critical in evaluating a library's success in achieving that vision. Knowing something about teens is the first step, and planning with the needs of teens in mind is the next. Knowing where we are and where we are going, we can collect the necessary data and move toward improving service to teens, which will in turn improve our libraries and our communities.

References

ACT for Youth Center of Excellence. 2002. "Adolescent Brain Development." *ACT for Youth Upstate Center of Excellence Research Facts and Findings*, May. http://www.actforyouth .net/resources/rf/rf_brain_0502.pdf.

Braun, Linda W. 2010. "The Importance of a Whole Library Approach to Public Library Young Adult Services: A YALSA Issue Paper." American Library Association. http://www.ala.org/ yalsa/guidelines/whitepapers/wholelibrary.

Chelton, Mary K. 2011. "Roots and Branches: YA Services Past, Present and Future." Young Adult Library Services Association. http://yalsa.ala.org/blog/wp-content/uploads/2011/ 01/2011_past_presidents_lecture_chelton.pdf.

Giedd, Jay. 2002. "Inside the Teenage Brain" (Interview). PBS. http://www.pbs.org/wgbh/pages/ frontline/shows/teenbrain/interviews/giedd.html.

Juskalian, Russ. 2010. "The Kids Can't Help It." *Newsweek*, December 26, 2010. http://www .newsweek.com/2010/12/16/the-kids-can-t-help-it.html.

Pew Research Center. 2010. "Millennials: A Portrait of Generation Next." Pew Research Center. http://pewresearch.org/millennials/.

Rainie, Lee. 2009. "Teens in the Digital Age." Pew Internet & American Life Project. http://www.slideshare.net/PewInternet/teens-in-digital-age.

Search Institute. 2006. "40 Developmental Assets® for Adolescents (Ages 12–18)." Search Institute. http://www.search-institute.org/system/files/40AssetsList.

Strauch, Barbara. 2003. *The Primal Teen.* New York: Doubleday.

Wikipedia, 2012. "Erikson's Stages of Psychosocial Development." Wikimedia Foundation. Last modified January 29. http://en.wikipedia.org/wiki/Erikson's_stages_of_psychosocial _development.

2
Planning

Developing Effective Goals and Objectives

Before beginning to collect data to evaluate programs and services, it is important to know why and what you are evaluating. Evaluation itself is not the goal; rather, the focus of evaluation should be on improvement: how to improve the services you offer, how to work smarter, and how to have the best possible library programs and services that improve the lives of not only teens but your whole community.

Evaluation can be perceived of as threatening by staff, who may assume that its purpose is to increase their workload, criticize them, or even eliminate their jobs. But if done well, evaluation can serve as an excellent tool for communication. Staff, administration, funders, board members, and other stakeholders should all be part of—or at least aware of—the evaluation process and should learn about its results. As Rhea Rubin says, "Most staff will be energized by the evidence that their work matters and makes a difference in people's lives" (Rubin, 2006: 13).

One way to start is by asking yourself what it is that you want to learn. For example, you may want to know:

- How can we get more teens into the library?
- How can we keep the teens who are here busy?
- Do we have good staff/teen interactions?
- Are we satisfying the reference/readers advisory needs of teens?
- Are we teaching teens how to use our resources?
- Do we have the right materials for teens, in the right quantities?
- Do we want to help teens with literacy, school success, career choices, recreational reading/listening/viewing (or all of the above)?
- Are teens making a positive impact in our community through library programs?
- Are teens doing better in school because of library resources and programs?
- Are teens involved at every stage of planning and presenting young adult programs and services?
- Are library staff members well versed in teen literature, adolescent development, and new technologies?

In evaluating your programs and services, you may have more than one audience in mind. That's fine, but it may mean that you need to collect different types of data for different people. Ideally, a library's overall teen services program will serve teens in a way that not only pleases them and helps them grow but also creates a healthier, safer community. But while teens may be more interested in knowing how many gaming programs you offer each year, or whether you subscribe to a certain magazine, or how quickly they can get the newest installment of their favorite series, your library board may be more interested in hearing about how many hours of community service teens performed at the library, or that using the library's databases for homework help has resulted in improved grades for high school students in your community. Your branch manager's goal may be to increase the circulation of young adult materials in the branch because that will mean that she gets a larger portion of the system's budget for next year. Each of your stakeholders may measure success differently, so you will want to identify who those stakeholders are and what it is that you want to tell them.

Outcome Measures

One way to evaluate the success of one's programs is to use outcome-based measurement. Outcome measurement is a form of evaluation that focuses on the question: "What difference did our program make to the participant?" (Rubin, 2006: 13). Put more simply, outcome measurement answers the question, "So what?" Outcomes are identified as quantifiable changes in the knowledge, skills, attitudes, behaviors, or status of the participant. This form of evaluation definitely requires thinking about the goals and objectives before you start. It isn't enough to say that your goal is to have 50 teens attend an SAT prep workshop at the library; that's not a result that has any impact on the participants of the workshop. An outcome statement might be that 80 percent of the teens who attend an SAT prep workshop will improve their SAT score by at least 100 points.

Outcome measurement requires planning. In order to measure changes in attitudes and behaviors, it is necessary to know where you started, and how that changed as a result of your program or service. In Chapter 4, we will look more at outcome-based evaluation.

Collecting Data: Types and Sources

One of the first steps in evaluating programs and services is collecting data and information about them. There are many ways to collect data. Numerical data, or statistics, are important, and we will look at some ways to gather, analyze, and use that type of data. It is also important to gather more subjective types of data, including information about what your users want and how they use the library, as well as information about the library's policies and strategic plan, and how they affect teen services.

Some types of data are relatively easy to collect, and it is always a good idea to start by taking a look at the data that your library already collects. In many cases these will be standard input and output measures (materials expenditures, circulation, etc.). There may also be other types of data, however: results of needs assessments and other surveys, for example.

There are very few national-level surveys of libraries that focus on young adults. In 1994, the National Center for Education Statistics (NCES) surveyed libraries and reported that 58 percent of (public) libraries housed young adult (YA) materials separately from other types of library materials, and that while young adults (aged 12–18) comprised 24 percent of library users, only 11 percent of libraries had a dedicated young adult librarian (NCES, 1995).

This had changed dramatically by the time of the Public Library Data Service (PLDS) survey in 2007. This collaboration between the Public Library Association (PLA) and the Young Adult Library Services Association (YALSA) was the first nationwide survey of young adult services since the 1995 NCES survey. The PLDS survey indicated that 85 percent of responding libraries had a separate young adult services department. Generally speaking, the larger the library, the more likely it was to have a separate young adult department. About 62 percent of libraries in the PLDS survey indicated that they have at least one young adult staff person, up from 11 percent in 1995. Similarly, the PLDS survey showed that about 84 percent of main libraries and 72 percent of branches housed teen materials in a separate area from children's or adult materials (PLA, 2007).

The PLDS survey is an excellent source of even more detailed information about young adult services in public libraries. In 2012, PLDS will again ask libraries about young adult services, and this will be an opportunity to have even more numbers for comparison.

In addition to the responses—by library—to each question, the final report includes some comparison charts: circulation of young adult materials per young adult, organized by size of service area; young adult materials expenditures per young adult, organized by size of service area; and young adult materials expenditures as a percentage of total materials expenditure. These charts can help an individual library determine where it fits in the spectrum of young adult services. We will return to some of these charts and statistics in Chapter 4, when we discuss analyzing and using the data.

Starting with statistical data, there are many types of information that are readily available, and it is always easiest to begin with existing reports.

User Data

This is information about the individuals who actually use the library, as well as information about the people in the library's legal service area. It can be valuable to learn where those two groups overlap. User data is usually available only in the aggregate, in order to maintain the privacy of individual users. Some of the data will be available from your library's integrated library system (ILS); other data may come from outside sources. Various types of census and demographic information are available. The U.S. Census (http://www.census.gov/) is a good starting place. The Census Bureau has begun to release data from the 2010 Census, and more will be released over the next few years. Another source for general demographic information is the Pew Internet & American Life Project (http://www.pewinternet.org/), particularly their ongoing survey of the Millennial generation, which includes today's teens (http://pewresearch.org/millennials/).

The U.S. Department of Education (http://www.ed.gov/), state departments of education, NCES (http://nces.ed.gov/), and local school districts are other sources for information on school-aged children. The Library Research Service (http://www.lrs.org/), a good source of information about libraries, includes links to library statistics from the states, as well as to school library statistics. Statewide library statistics can be very useful for comparative purposes, but for the most part young adult collections, programs, and circulation are not called out as separate categories. They are generally included as part of adult statistics.

National statistics and averages can be useful, but specific local information is the most likely to be able to help you tailor your programs and services to the needs of your community. Local school district demographics are going to tell you more about the teens in your community than a nationwide survey of teens. City, county, and regional census information will be focused more precisely on your community and its makeup. Some libraries regularly (or occasionally) conduct community surveys and community needs assessments. These usually not only include detailed demographic information about a community but also summarize findings of surveys and focus groups that describe the kinds of things that members of the community are looking for in community services in general and the library in particular.

You do need to know what your service area is and who your users are. These may not be the same thing. It may be simple: a city, town, county, or school district. However, library districts are often complicated. In many areas of the country, for example, there may be a county library that services the smaller towns and unincorporated areas, while the larger cities in the county have their own municipal libraries. Library users usually ignore those distinctions and go wherever it is most convenient for them. So your actual users may not all live in your official service area. Most of your official statistical data is going to focus on the legal service area residents, although circulation data will reflect the actual users of your library. This can produce skewed statistics. For example, if your library is in a small town, its legal service area may be the residents of the town. However, if there is a much larger town nearby, and its residents frequently use your library because of its location or because of its excellent collection or programs, your use statistics will show a higher than expected count of circulation per resident.

Usage Data

Every library collects vast amounts of circulation data. This is one of the great benefits of automated circulation systems. Data can be collected and formatted in many different ways, and it can be extremely beneficial to do so. In later chapters, we will explore some of the ways you can format and analyze data to help you evaluate your programs and services. Circulation data can tell you how many items of various types have been checked out over a particular period of time. They can tell you, in general terms, who has checked out items.

Information about your library's collection is also available from your automated circulation system. It is useful to do comparative analysis between the circulation data and the collection data. For example, compare the percentage of the collection that is young adult materials to the percentage of circulation created by those same materials. Or create a report that shows how many times, on average, young adult materials circulate in a given year. This can be narrowed by category: books, DVDs, games, audio materials, and so on. This data should also include electronic collections—e-books and journals, electronic databases, and so on. In Chapter 3, we will look at some ways to analyze circulation and collection information.

Other usage statistics have to do with both the physical and virtual presences of the library. For example, most libraries collect information on the number of visits per day, or per open hour. There are also snapshot reports, such as the seat occupancy rate at different hours. For the library's virtual presence, most systems count the number of log-ins, the number of unique log-ins, the number of downloads of electronic books and journals, and so on. In almost all cases, while these measures may give an idea of the library's overall usage, it is not possible to single out usage by young adults.

Policies and Procedures

The library's policies and procedures are an often-overlooked source of data that can be very useful in evaluating programs and services. Most libraries have written policies regarding everything from behavior to checkout limits and more. Before you begin to evaluate young adult services and programs, read these policies and note which ones affect those services.

A good place to start is a library's strategic plan, mission, values, and goals. These documents may give you an idea of whether the library has an institutional commitment to serving teens. In many cases, however, teens will be included in a phrase like "all users" or "every member of the community." Strategic planning usually involves some sort of community needs assessment process. Finding out whether programs and services for teens were specifically mentioned in that process will let you know something about their priority in the community. You can look at these documents from the perspective of serving teens and determine whether the wording of the mission and values seems appropriate for teens, and whether teens are specifically called out as a service priority. If a library's strategic plan does not include goals that are specific to teen services, it may be that they can be developed.

When you look at the library's policies and procedures, you can also do so from the perspective of serving teens. Here are some suggestions for the type of information you can cull from policies:

- Are there separate policies regarding the behavior of teens in the library? For example, some libraries have policies limiting the number of people who may sit at one table or congregate around one computer, and this type of policy is usually aimed (implicitly if not explicitly) at controlling loud and boisterous teen behavior.
- Does your library require parental permission for minors to access certain parts of the collection?
- Are there different borrowing periods or fines for the use of teen materials?
- Does the library have policies regarding computer and Internet access that are different for children, teens, and adults?
- Does the collection development policy include mention of teen collections?
- Does the library's collection development policy require two positive reviews from standard library sources before an item can be purchased? This one policy can preclude the purchase of many popular teen materials.
- Does the library need new policies that address issues relating to teen services and programs?

This is a big area of evaluation, and it may take a lot more time than merely analyzing some statistics. In Chapter 3, we will look a little more deeply at ways in which you can analyze policies, procedures, and strategic plans and use them to support high-quality teen services.

Program Data

The most basic program statistic, and the one that almost everyone collects, is attendance. But even in collecting attendance numbers, there are ways to do it that will help you later analyze your programs and fine-tune them. You can simply count the number of bodies in the room. You can categorize attendees by age: How many are from the target age group and how many are older or younger? Are you counting parents or other adults who attend YA programs? For programs such as gaming or craft programs, where attendees may move from station to station, you may want to take a "snapshot" of attendance every 15 or 30 minutes. In the case of a two-hour gaming program, you might take periodic counts of how many attendees are playing on the Wii, how many are watching, how many are at computer stations, how many are playing board games, and so on. There will be a natural movement from station to station over the two hours. Attendees may start at the Wii (either watching or playing), then move to the board games only after they have had their turn on the electronic games. If you only count at the beginning of the session, you may be led to believe that no one is interested in the board games.

And it's not only about the numbers of attendees. You may want to find out if a gaming program, for example, brought in teens who have never been to the library before. You can also use program attendees as an informal focus group and get some input on the library's collections and services. By asking them to fill out an evaluation form before they leave, you can solicit recommendations for library materials and future programs.

Collecting information from teens can be a challenge, but it will pay off in the long run. In *Connecting Young Adults and Libraries*, Gorman and Suellentrop (2009) point out: "Teens will answer the questions put in front of them, but if you don't ask the right questions you may never receive the most useful comments" (p. 258). Besides collecting information from participants, library staff who worked on the program need to document staff time required to plan, promote, and present the program as well as costs incurred in the program (supplies, food, promotional materials, presenters, etc.). Collecting data as you go along, and keeping it on file, is the only good way to obtain this type of information, which can prove invaluable later on. We will discuss program evaluations in more detail in Chapter 4.

Budget Data

Knowing how a library budgets its resources is a strong hint as to how it prioritizes services and programs. There are a few basic things to know about library budgets. First, public libraries and public schools are by definition public, which means that their budgets must be approved by some public entity (a city, a county, a library district) in a public forum. Second, for almost all libraries, the largest portion of the budget goes to personnel. This is usually from one-half to three-quarters of any library's operating budget and includes salaries and benefits for everyone who works for the library. The second largest portion of the budget is usually operating expenses, which includes everything from rent and utilities to toilet paper and pencils. Equipment, including the ever more critical electronic equipment, may be included as an operating expense, or it may be considered a capital expense. For example, if your library has a plan to replace all of the library's computers every five years, money may be set aside in a capital equipment account each year, so that it is available in a lump sum when it is time to make that large purchase.

In setting the personnel budget, libraries must determine how many people in each employee classification they will have. As part of the budgeting process, a library may or may not delineate specific areas of responsibility for employees. That is, the library budget may simply indicate that there will be five librarians, not that there will be two adult services librarians, two children's services librarians, and one teen services librarian. However, this information may be available at a finer level of detail and is a piece of data worth having when analyzing a library's commitment to teen services.

Although it is personnel-related, training and continuing education is usually part of the operations budget. Finding out whether there is a training budget, how much it is, and how it is allocated will tell you something about the library's priorities.

The materials budget is another area of great interest in terms of teen services. Although books and other library materials are also an operating expense, most libraries list materials expenditures as a separate budget line item. State library statistics require that libraries indicate how much of the materials budget goes to adult materials and how much to children's. Young adult materials are counted as part of adult materials for the purposes of most states. Therefore, individual libraries may not have a separate line item for young adult materials. Again, however, it is worthwhile to find out whether your library calls out young adult materials as a separate item, and to look at how that figure compares to the numbers for children's and adult materials. In many libraries, teen recreational materials—mainly fiction—may be bought out of the young adult budget, while curriculum support materials are purchased—and shelved—as part of the children's and/or adult budget. Likewise, electronic databases that serve the homework help needs of teens and downloadable audio and e-books may be purchased out of the adult budget or a separate database budget.

If a separate teen materials budget exists, you will want to determine if and how it is subdivided. Is it one lump sum, or is it divided between books and media? Are there separate lines for graphic novels, comic books, magazines, paperbacks, nonfiction, music, video games, and so forth?

This level of detail is not likely to be included in the budget that is presented to the library's governing authority, but it will be somewhere because someone in the library will be tracking the library's expenditures. It may be the library director or assistant director, a budget director, a collection development manager, or an adult or children's services manager. Libraries have different titles for these roles, and a lot will depend upon the size of the library. In a small public library, the director may be responsible for every aspect of the budget. In a large system, responsibility will naturally be more spread out. In many automated library systems, acquisitions are tracked much as circulation and collection are tracked, and it is a case of finding out who has the authority to look at those numbers, and who can create reports that will help you evaluate expenditures.

Facilities Data

The physical environment in which library service takes place is another area in which you can collect data. Often, this is relatively simply observable data. For example, you can start by measuring the size of your building and the size of various areas and collections:

- Total square footage of building
- Square footage of area designated for young adults
- For comparison, square footage of areas designated for other groups (children, adults, seniors, etc.)
- Shelving (by square footage or by shelving units) for young adult materials
- For comparison, shelving for other groups
- Total number of seats in building (lounge seating, seats at computers, seats at desks, tables, or carrels)
- Seats in young adult area

In addition to counting and measuring, you may want to observe other factors in the physical environment, and determine where the young adult area fits into the larger picture of the library. For example, look at questions of safety, lighting, temperature, noise, cleanliness, and so on. Do areas that are designated for or frequented by young adults have the same level of lighting and cleanliness as other areas of the library, for example? Are there computers in the teen area, and are there different types of seating? Are there places where teens can study in groups? Are there listening stations, places to plug in laptops, and places to recharge mobile devices?

Of course, all of these questions assume that the facility is able to be used by teens. How many hours is the library open each week? Are these hours that are convenient for teens? If the library closes every day at 5 p.m., usage by teens is going to be limited because they are in school most of the hours the library is open. And perhaps your library offers outreach services to teens in schools, such as booktalking and database training.

Function Data

Measuring library functions can be more complicated than simply finding numbers on a report. Library functions include the many things that make a library work well (or not so well) for its users, but which can be difficult to quantify. Here are some examples:

- **Materials selection:** Beyond the dollar amount spent on young adult materials, are the right materials being selected? Is the collection meeting the needs of the population? Is teen input solicited and used in selection? Are the appropriate formats being collected, and are the appropriate selection tools being used?
- **Acquisition:** If a teen requests an item that the library doesn't own, is it acquired in a timely manner? Are there policies or procedures in place that slow down the acquisition of materials that are not reviewed in mainstream library publications or available from standard jobbers? How long does it take from the moment an order is placed to the moment it is in the hand of a user?

- **Organization and access:** Is it easy to find materials in the collection? Can teens find the items they want on their own, or is staff mediation required? Do separate collections (e.g., series paperbacks, test prep, career materials) make it easier or harder for teens to find the materials they want? Is the catalog accurate?
- **Services:** Do teens have the same access to reference and readers' advisory services as adults and children? Are staff members prepared to deal with the unique types of queries that teens bring to the reference desk?
- **Outreach:** Does the library offer programs in local schools? Does the library offer programs for teens in nontraditional settings, including detention facilities? Does the library provide access to materials through the mail or delivery to schools or other agencies?

Staffing Data

Besides budget questions of the number and type of staff assigned to the library in general and the teen area in particular, there are other types of information to collect about the library's commitment to staff:

- Does the library offer training for all staff who interact with teens in the library?
- Does this include training on adolescent development? What types of training and how many hours per year?
- What is the library's policy on continuing education? Are staff members encouraged to take courses, attend conferences, etc.? Are these paid for? Is continuing education tracked?
- Are staff provided with the tools they need to work with teens? Are there library subscriptions to professional journals, including *Young Adult Library Services*, *School Library Journal*, *Booklist*, and *Voice of Youth Advocates*? Are these routed in a timely manner to all staff who select materials for or otherwise work with teens?
- Does the library recruit and encourage teen volunteers? Are teens allowed to do school-mandated community service hours at the library? Who supervises teen volunteers? Are teens included in developing and presenting programs?
- Are librarians and other library workers who prepare programs and select materials for teens given off-desk time for these tasks? What is the ratio of on-desk to off-desk hours?
- Does the library have any system in place for administration or the public to measure the quality of service provided by staff, or staff helpfulness?

Finding Data

As noted earlier, some of the information discussed in this chapter will be easy to find. Some will be in existing reports, and some will be accessible by creating custom reports in the library's automated system. Some will be available through relatively simple observations and measurements. Some may require creating new instruments to collect data, such as surveys, focus groups, interviews, or suggestion forms. As we discuss in Chapter 3 some of the ways to analyze the data, and as you determine what your evaluation goals are, you will gain a better understanding of which data you want to collect.

Chapter 6 includes some checklists to help you determine the areas in your library that need particular attention.

References

Gorman, Michele, and Tricia Suellentrop. 2009. *Connecting Young Adults and Libraries: A How-to-Do-It Manual*, 4th ed. New York: Neal-Schuman.

NCES (National Center for Education Statistics). 1995. "Services and Resources for Children and Young Adults in Public Libraries." National Center for Education Statistics. http://nces.ed.gov/surveys/frss/publications/95357/.

PLA (Public Library Association). 2007. *Public Library Data Service Statistical Report 2007*. Chicago: Public Library Association.

Rubin, Rhea Joyce, for the Public Library Association. 2006. *Demonstrating Results: Using Outcome Measurement in Your Library*. Chicago: American Library Association.

3

Implementation

Raw Data: What Does It Mean?

Now that you have collected mountains of data, what do you do with it? How do you use it to evaluate your program and, beyond that, to make changes and plan for the future? As noted in Chapter 2, it is not enough merely to have statistics. Statistics and measurement are an important part of evaluation, but only a part. First, your data need to be accurate. Second, you need to understand what they represent. Every integrated library system (ILS) is a little different, and every library sets up its reports in its own way. The more time you spend with reports and statistics, the better you will understand what is actually being collected. Third, you need to analyze the data. This probably means organizing it in different ways than the way it came out of the ILS. Fourth, you need to interpret the data. You can make comparisons to benchmarks, look at changes over time, compare statistical data to information obtained from word-of-mouth or other subjective surveys, and so on. Finally, to make any of the work worthwhile, you must communicate and use the information.

All of this takes time and energy, but it is not terribly complicated. In fact, once you start delving into the reports and playing around with graphs and charts, it can be very absorbing. Better yet, having the information at your fingertips can make all the difference when it is time for decisions to be made. Having real facts and figures to back up your gut instincts can go a long way in helping you to get changes made in your library and in improving the services you offer.

Statistical Data

Start with the statistical data you collected and make a few basic calculations. For example, look at the user data you collected. These measures and ratios are known as input measures and output measures. There are also satisfaction- or results-based outcome measures. But what they are called is not as important as what they tell you and how you use them.

Input Measures and Output Measures

Input measures tell you what you have to work with: population, budget, collections, staff, and space. One example of an important input measure is the number of teens in your service area, and another is the overall population of your service area. Once you know those two numbers, you can do a simple calculation to learn what percentage of the service area population is in this age group.

# of teens in service area ÷ total population of service area = %

This will give you a baseline percentage that you can use in making comparisons. Other input measures or baseline numbers that will be useful to you are in Table 3.1.

Output measures tell you how the library is being used: circulation, collection use, visits, reference questions, and so on. The circulation of teen materials and the circulation of materials by teen cardholders are important output measures to track and compare. Other examples of output measures can be seen in Table 3.2.

So, for example, if you learn that teens make up 18 percent of your service area, you can use that number in comparing other things. What percentage of the budget goes to teen services? What percentage of circulation comes from teen materials? What percentage of the collection do teen materials represent? What percentage of library cardholders are teens?

Here are some ways to look at this information. Figure 3.1 shows a public library's registered borrowers by age. Most state library statistical reports ask for information about children, 14 and younger, and lump teens in with adults. In the case shown here, the ILS records registered borrowers by birth year. By entering the data into a spreadsheet program, such as Microsoft Excel, it is possible to sort the users in any way desired. In this case, they were sorted by adults (19 and older), teens (12–18), and children (11 and younger). So 75 percent of the registered borrowers are adults, 11 percent are teens, and 14 percent are children.

In this community, let's assume that 70 percent of residents are adults, 8 percent are teens, and 22 percent are children. So the percentages of borrowers are not too far off from the community profile. In many cases, parents get library cards so they can check out materials for their young children, so it is reasonable to see a lower percentage of children borrowers than children in the community.

Next, when we look at materials borrowed from this library, we see in Figure 3.2 that adult materials make up 47 percent of the library's circulation, children's materials are 44 percent, and teen materials are 9 percent. When analyzing these numbers, it is important to look at the big picture. Why is it that 14 percent of borrowers are children, but 44 percent of circulation is of children's items? There could be several explanations, and it is likely a combination of factors. For one thing, adults often check out items for their children—either because their children are too young for their own cards, or to keep track of the items more easily. Another possibility is that children's items, especially books, tend to be shorter. A parent might think nothing of checking out a

Table 3.1. Input Measures

Measure	Definition
Number of teen cardholders	Count the number of teens (using your library's age definition, e.g., 12–18)
Percent of teen cardholders (calculate also for adult and child cardholders)	# of teen cardholders ÷ Total # of cardholders
Percent of teens in service area	# of teens in service area ÷ Total number of people in service area
Teen materials budget as percent of the total	Teen materials budget ÷ Total materials budget
Teen materials budget per capita	Teen materials budget ÷ # of teen cardholders
Percent of teen materials less than three years old	# of items purchased in the last three years ÷ Total number of items in the (teen) collection
Number of staff assigned to teen services (also calculate for adult, children's services)	Use full-time equivalent of librarians plus paraprofessionals
Number of teen staff per capita	Teen staff FTE ÷ Teen population
Population served per staff member	Teen population ÷ Teen Staff FTE
Total number of titles (and volumes) owned	Count the titles (and volumes) in the teen collection
Percent of items on loan	Total number of items from the teen collection that are checked out ÷ Total number owned
Items in the teen collection per capita	Items in the teen collection ÷ Teen cardholders
Total library floor space	Expressed in square feet
Floor space designated for teens (also calculate for adults, children)	Expressed in square feet
Percent of library designated for teens (also calculate for adults, children)	Total floor space ÷ Floor space designated for teens
Number of seats in library	Count lounge chairs, chairs at tables, desks, carrels, and computer stations
Number of seats in teen area (also calculate for adults, children)	Count lounge chairs, chairs at tables, desks, carrels, and computer stations
Percent of library seats that are in the teen area (also calculate for children's area)	Number of seats in teen area ÷ Total number of seats in library
Teen program attendance (also calculate for preschool and school-age children)	Number of individuals attending teen programs annually
Programs for teens (also calculate for preschool and school-age children)	Number of programs annually

Table 3.2. Output Measures

Measure	Definition
Total library circulation	Number of items checked out annually
Teen materials circulation (also calculate for children's and adult items)	Number of items checked out annually that are designated as teen collections
Circulation per capita	Total circulation ÷ Total population of service area
Teen materials circulation per capita	Teen materials circulation ÷ Teen cardholders or Teen population of service area
Circulation by material type	Materials borrowed, separated by category (fiction, nonfiction, graphic novels, DVDs, etc.)
Turnover rate of teen materials	Annual circulation of teen materials ÷ Number of items in teen collection
Seat occupancy rate (snapshot—do at different times of day and week)	Number of chairs being used ÷ Total number of seats available
Circulation by teens (also calculate for children, adults)	Number of items checked out annually by teen borrowers
Percent of teen circulation	Circulation by teens ÷ Total circulation

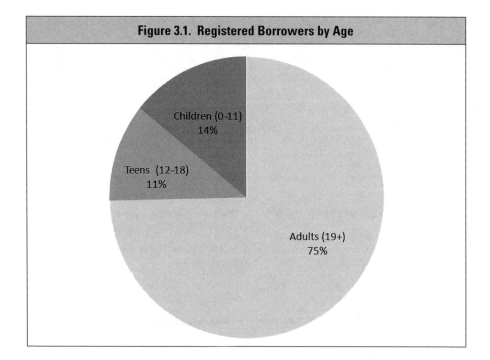

Figure 3.1. Registered Borrowers by Age

Children (0–11) 14%

Teens (12–18) 11%

Adults (19+) 75%

dozen picture books at once but would only check out one or two adult books at a time. A dozen picture books could easily be read—and reread—within a normal borrowing period of two to three weeks, while one adult novel might require the entire time. Borrowing periods are another factor to look at: is the borrowing period for all items the same? A large portion of the children's circulation may come from DVDs, which have a one-week checkout period, while more of adult circulation comes from books, with a three-week checkout period.

In this example, teens are 11 percent of borrowers, and teen materials account for 9 percent of circulation. This seems reasonable if we consider that teens for the most part check out their own materials, rather than parents doing it for them. As with adults, the materials they check out are longer. Added to that is the fact that teens are in middle school or high school, and their schoolwork and extracurricular activities often limit the amount of outside reading, listening, or viewing they can do. Also, teens check out materials from other areas of the collection. They frequently use both adult and children's nonfiction to complete school assignments, and they read for pleasure from all areas of the library. So teen cardholders account for circulation of teen, adult, and children's materials. You can test this theory by running a report that counts number of items checked out by teens in each of the library's collection codes. In the examples shown in Figures 3.3 and 3.4, teens on average check out about a third of their materials from the adult collection, a third from teen, and a third from

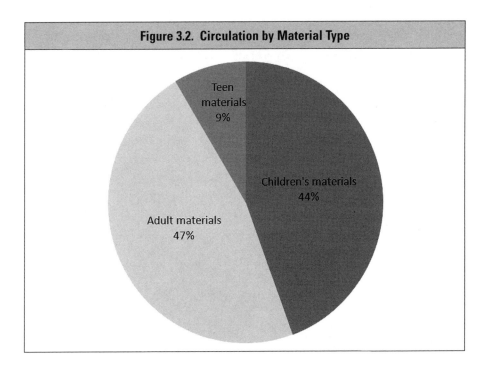

Figure 3.2. Circulation by Material Type

Teen materials 9%

Children's materials 44%

Adult materials 47%

children's. As might be expected, however, younger teens check out more items from the children's collection, and older teens check out more items from the adult collection. In this example, the peak use for teen materials is among 14- to 15-year-olds. Knowing this information could be useful in evaluating the collection: is the collection weighted toward items that appeal to these ages, or should more items for this age group be purchased for the collection because they are the heaviest users?

If the situation were different—if, for example, teens were 11 percent of borrowers, but teen materials accounted for only 1 percent of circulation, further investigation would be required. Are teens coming to the library (we know they have cards), but not checking materials out? Do they have cards only so they can use the Internet? Are they getting all of their curriculum-based materials either online or at their school library? Do they have an exceptional school library that provides them with ample recreational reading material? Is this a wealthy community where every teen has access to an e-reader and an endless supply of e-books? These are questions that statistics alone cannot tell you. In this case, the statistics merely point you to the places where you need to use further means of evaluation: surveys, focus groups, or other subjective data-collection instruments.

Another possibility in the earlier scenario is that the teen collection is simply inappropriate to the needs of the local teens, and they are all checking out materials from the adult or children's collection. It might be possible to go back to your data to

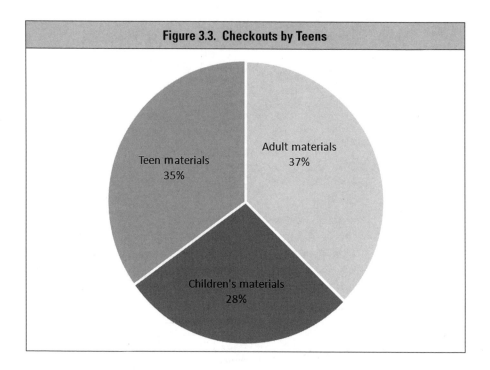

Figure 3.3. Checkouts by Teens

Teen materials
35%

Adult materials
37%

Children's materials
28%

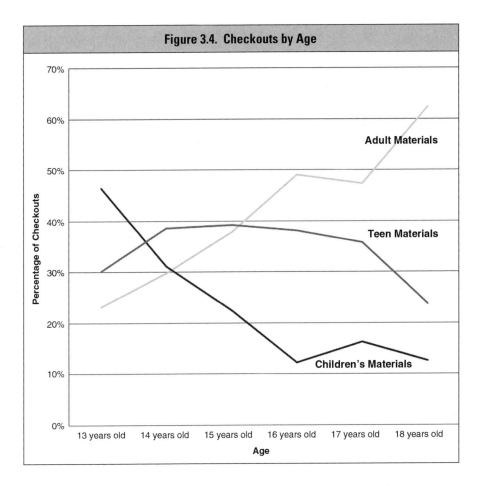

Figure 3.4. Checkouts by Age

explore this possibility further, by running a report that shows what types of items were checked out, sorted by birth year of the user. This, however, might be an example of the kind of report that would require special programming. If it is not a basic report that the library ILS offers, there might be expense involved in creating it, and the library would have to decide whether the information received is worth the expense.

Turnover is a measure of the typical use of a particular collection over the course of a given period of time. Calculating the turnover rate gives an idea of how well the collection as a whole or any specific part of it is circulating. Turnover is also a good predictor of future use. To calculate turnover, determine the number of items you have in the teen collection and in any subcollections. This will depend on how your collection codes are assigned in your ILS. For example, look at Table 3.3.

In this collection, there are 5,217 items in the fiction collection, divided among fiction, science fiction, mystery, short stories, and paperbacks. Based on the annual circulation for each of those areas, fiction books circulate an average of 5.62 times per

Table 3.3. Turnover			
	Number of Items	Yearly Circulation	Yearly Turnover Rate
Teen Fiction	1,720	12,054	7.01
Teen Science Fiction	482	2,316	4.80
Teen Paperbacks	2,941	14,734	5.01
Teen Mystery	38	94	2.47
Teen Short Stories	36	130	3.61
Total Teen Fiction	**5,217**	**29,328**	**5.62**
Teen Nonfiction	1,561	3,170	2.03
Teen Graphic Novels	1,855	16,154	8.71
Teen Audiobooks	322	1,318	4.09
Teen Music CDs	1,423	16,168	11.36
Teen DVDs	153	1,702	11.12
Total	**10,531**	**67,840**	**6.44**

year, with straight fiction circulating most at 7.01 times per item, and mysteries least at 2.47 times per item. Of course, these numbers are just averages for a collection. In a fiction collection, for example, some titles—such as the newest, hottest series—will circulate 12–15 times a year or more, depending on the library's circulation period. Other older items will languish on the shelves and circulate once, twice, or not at all.

It is worth noting here that collection data are always going to be a snapshot in time. Your ILS can tell you that on this day at the moment the report was run, there were 2,941 items in this particular collection code. The next minute, items might have added to or deleted from the system, collection codes might have been changed, entire sections might have been weeded. Collection data can give you an overview, but they are most useful when examined over time, to see how collections grow and decline. Nevertheless, in conjunction with circulation data, collection reports can tell you important things about what is happening in your library.

Looking at Table 3.3, it is clear that DVDs, CDs, and graphic novels are the most popular items in the collection. This seems to fit what we know about the viewing, listening, and reading interests of teens. If this is a typical public library, however, we also know that not only teens check out these items. Popular music CDs, even if they are shelved in the teen area, may be checked out by adults and children alike.

Another useful type of report for analyzing a collection is an aging report. In many cases, the ILS can create this report automatically. Table 3.4 is an example of an aging report. In this collection, almost all items are under ten years old, and almost three-quarters are under five years old. This library obviously has a commitment to maintaining a collection of attractive new books and other materials.

The table does prompt some questions and some speculation. For example, it is important to understand how the aging report is created. In this case, the numbers indicate the age of the actual item, not its copyright date. In other words, the library may own copies of S. E. Hinton's *The Outsiders*, Robert Cormier's *The Chocolate War*, and Nancy Garden's *Annie on My Mind*, but they are not the original versions, published in the 1960s, 1970s, and 1980s. They are newer copies of the same books. Why would this be the case? There could be several reasons. This might be a relatively new library, with an opening-day collection of newly purchased items. It might be a well-funded library that has a commitment to replacing worn and tattered copies on a regular

Table 3.4. Aging Report											
Item Circ Type	**0–1 year**		**2–5 years**		**6–10 years**		**11–20 years**		**21+ years**		**UNK Age**	**TOTAL**
Teen CD Rock	231	16%	472	33%	370	25%	279	21%				1,352
Teen CD Talking Book	100	75%	24	18%	10	7%						134
Teen DVD Nonfeature	25	19%	74	55%	35	26%						134
Teen Fiction	333	43%	256	33%	145	19%	37	5%	1	0%		772
Teen Mystery	0	0%	11	30%	0	0%	10	27%	16	43%		37
Teen Nonfiction	123	14%	489	56%	231	26%	36	4%				879
Teen Nonfiction Graphic Novel	322	97%	10	3%	0	0%						332
Teen Paperback	376	19%	1,241	62%	389	19%						2,006
Teen Science Fiction	130	66%	21	11%	45	23%	1	1%				197
Teen Short Story	5	22%	18	78%	0	0%						23
	1,645	28%	2,616	45%	1,225	21%	363	6%	17	0%		5,866

basis. It might be a library with a high theft rate, in which new copies are purchased to replace stolen ones. Again, the numbers themselves don't tell the whole story.

Looking at the categories themselves also leads to some questions. The category "Teen Mystery" shows no new items, but 16 in the 21+ age range. This is worth examining. Are teen mysteries no longer being written or being purchased by the library, or has the library simply decided that the category is no longer relevant? Similarly, the fact that there are 322 graphic novels in the 0–1 year category, only ten in the 2–5 years category, and none older than that would indicate that graphic novels are a new collection: either they were never collected before the past few years, or they were somehow categorized differently before that.

As noted in Chapter 1, some of these reports may be regular reports that the library's ILS runs. However, pulling out information specific to teen users or teen materials may require some more effort. In some cases, it may be possible to ask the library's system staff to run a specific report that isolates exactly the information needed. In other cases, it may be necessary to pull data out of a larger report and create a specialized report in Microsoft Excel or some other spreadsheet program. But it is worthwhile to think about what kinds of information would be useful in analyzing your collection and circulation and finding out if and how those reports are available.

Another number that can be useful is the number or percentage of the collection that has been checked out in the past year (or two, or whatever time period you like). This, like turnover, will give you an idea of how active your collection is. Reports of specific titles that have not been checked out recently can also tell you two important things: which items just aren't going out, but also (if a title is on the list but not on the shelf) which items have been stolen. The items that are stolen are almost always ones that you want to buy more of, because of their popularity. It is also worthwhile to look at holds, or reserves. Knowing how many holds there are per copy of a popular book will give you a clue about when it is time to add more copies.

Evaluating Policies and Procedures

As noted in Chapter 2, most libraries have written policies and procedures, and the first step is to find out what those are. Policies and procedures are not written in a vacuum. Often they are written in response to particular circumstances or situations. Library workers tend to prefer avoiding confrontation and may find it easier to create a rule they can point to. The fact that teenagers often respond to a reprimand with a belligerent "Who says so?" or "There's no law against that" only adds to the desire to have everything in writing.

So, for example, it may be easier to have a policy that states "No more than four people at a table" than to approach a noisy group of eight teens and insist that they quiet down. In analyzing policies, it is often best to look at what you are trying to accomplish. What is the purpose of a policy that states "No more than four people at a table"? It is probably to keep the noise levels down because when six or eight or ten people are gathered around a four-person table, there tends to be noise, talking, laughter, shoving, and so on. So in analyzing the policy, the question is whether there are other ways to achieve the same goal. For example, some libraries state that skateboards are not permitted in the library. Some teens use their skateboards as a primary mode of transportation, and not allowing skateboards in the library means not allowing those teens in the library. But what is the goal? Most likely, the library wants to discourage the use of skateboards inside the library or on library grounds because it can be dangerous or disruptive. So instead, the policy might state something like this: "You may bring your skateboard, roller skates, or other sports equipment into the library while you look for materials, but they may not be used on library property."

In another example, some libraries prohibit moving or rearranging library furniture or equipment without specific, even signed, permission from library administration. This sounds like a policy that was created in response to a situation in which people (probably teens) moved a group of chairs into a more social seating arrangement or pushed some tables together so they could work on a project. The goal may be to discourage noise, or possibly to maintain clear walkways in the library. A possible response to this issue might be to have one or more areas in the library with flexible seating options—light chairs or cushions that can be moved around easily, for example, or a group study room, where tables can be moved as the users desire. Of course, space considerations can be limiting here, but it is usually possible to look for ways to achieve the goal without prohibiting all movement of furniture: "Only these chairs/tables may be moved, and they must remain within this area."

Policies surrounding circulation practices are another area to look at in terms of how teens are being served. Teens fall into a gray area in many libraries: they are still minors, but they have more autonomy than children. How circulation policies deal with teens may have a lot to do with where teen services fits into the library administratively. If teen services falls under the children's services or youth services department, policies for teens are apt to be more similar to policies for children. If teen services falls under adult services, the distinction between children and teens is apt to be greater.

Community values also play heavily into decisions about teens' access to materials. Teen access can be restricted in various ways. Some libraries require a parent or guardian to sign a release before a minor can receive a card. Some issue special "youth" or "under 18" cards that restrict borrowing to certain parts of the collection: no R-rated movies, for example, or only limited or filtered access to the Internet. Others make no distinctions at all—anyone can get a card, and there is no difference between a child's card and an adult's card. Children are permitted to borrow any item in the library. The Traverse Area District Library in Michigan states it very clearly in their policy manual: "As it is contrary to the Library's primary function of providing access to library media by individuals regardless of age, race, religion, national origin, or social political views, the Library cannot and will not establish or enforce any barrier to the materials in its collection based solely on the age of the patron" (TADL, 2003).

One question to examine about policies regarding library cards is the privacy of the cardholder. Everyone seems to agree that the records of adults are and should be private, but the line becomes grayer when it comes to minors. Parents often see themselves as responsible for the child's behavior, and so feel they have a right to know what the child is borrowing. A common statement from parents is something like, "Well, if I have to pay his overdue fines, then I need to know what he has checked out." One way around this issue is not to make parents responsible for a minor's fines.

Another barrier for young people in having access to the library is the requirements for obtaining a library card. If a government-issued photo ID is required, for example, this effectively excludes any young person who does not have a driver's license or a passport. A teen-friendly policy would include some options for younger users: a school identification card, for example. Some libraries have the applicant address a postcard to himself or herself at the registered address. The library mails the card, and once it is delivered, the applicant can bring it back to the library for proof of address.

Teens, of course, fall into an interesting gray area in all of these considerations. Teens are at a point in their lives when they want more privacy and have greater needs for information. In looking at a library's policies for minors, it is worth exploring the question of whether all policies that apply to the protection of children should also apply to teens. If a library does limit teens' access to materials, what is the basis of the limitation? It may be a state law, or the library attorney's interpretation of a law, or simply a decision by the library's board of trustees.

A good way to analyze and evaluate the policies in your library is to ask the teens who use the library. Teens have a keen sense of justice. As noted in Chapter 1, they are also learning to take responsibility for their own actions, so they are usually well aware of policies that discriminate—or appear to discriminate—against them. Working with teens to regulate the library's environment in a manner that seems fair and equitable is a good way to get buy-in from them on the rules and on the consequences for breaking the rules.

Competencies

Core competencies for librarians and library workers are focused on the individual who is providing service. Evaluating staff is a critical part of evaluating a library's effectiveness in serving teens, as we will see in Chapter 4, but having a competent staff is only part of the picture. Any evaluation of a library's teen services program is going to need to look at the competence of the people who are providing service.

The American Library Association (ALA) has created a set of "Core Competences of Librarianship." It is specific to "the basic knowledge to be possessed by all persons graduating from an ALA-accredited master's program in library and information studies." It focuses on the basics of the profession, stating: "Librarians working in school, academic, public, special, and governmental libraries, and in other contexts will need to possess specialized knowledge beyond that specified here" (ALA, 2009).

The Young Adult Library Services Association (YALSA) has created a set of competencies specifically aimed at librarians and library workers who serve teens. "YALSA's Competencies for Librarians Serving Youth: Young Adults Deserve the Best" (YALSA, 2010) is a good place to start looking at a library's commitment to serving teens. The competencies can serve as a framework for staff development and as a basis for advocacy for teen services. Competencies can be very useful in developing job descriptions and interview questions.

YALSA's competencies, for example, focus on seven areas in which librarians who serve teens should have proficiency:

1. Leadership and Professionalism includes advocacy, ethics, professional development, youth participation, mentoring, and building assets in youth.
2. Knowledge of the Client Group focuses on becoming familiar with the developmental needs of teens and with the kinds of resources and services needed and wanted by teens of all types.
3. Communication, Marketing, and Outreach focuses on promoting young adult services among teens, library staff, the community, and decision makers.
4. Administration discusses the skills needed to manage a young adult services program, including identifying resources, and involving teens in decision making.
5. Knowledge of Materials focuses on the importance of building a collection that is appropriate for teens.
6. Access to Information covers the areas of physical and virtual access, merchandizing, and intellectual freedom.
7. Services focuses on the wide variety of services that libraries provide for and with teens.

Again, these competencies are focused on individual library workers, particularly librarians. In Chapter 5 we will look at competencies in greater detail and discuss some ways they can be used to evaluate libraries and library workers.

Using Data to Make Changes

Analyzing data will inevitably lead to some conclusions. Suppose, for example, you conclude that circulation of teen materials is lower than you think it should be, based on the number of teens in the community and the number who have library cards.

The next step is to determine why that is the case. You can do this in several ways. You could ask the teens why they are not checking teen materials out from the library. Perhaps, as noted earlier, they are using their school library or buying what they need. Perhaps they are checking out materials from the library, just not teen materials.

One approach would be to compare circulation of teen materials with the aging report. If the teen collection trends to the older side, it might be that the collection is simply too old, ragged, and out-of-date to appeal to teens. Given an adequate budget, this is a simple hypothesis to test: weed the collection heavily and replace with new materials, and then check the circulation again.

Having the necessary information is the key. Ask yourself what you would need to tell your library director, or board of trustees, to convince them that the teen collection needs a great share of the materials budget, and then figure out how to get that information and how to share it with them. You can start from either direction: from the information that you already have or from the desired results. Just use the data you have been collecting to make a logical and defensible case and present it professionally.

Other types of changes can also result from careful evaluation. Evaluating not only the teen responses to your programs, but the time and money the library puts into creating them, can help you determine if the programs are worthwhile, or if you need to go in a different direction. If your evaluation reveals, for example, that you are reaching the same group of 20 teens with all of your programs, it might be time to consider whether your resources would be better spent in reaching out to underserved teens in the community.

Changing Policies

If in analyzing a library's policies and procedures, you conclude that changes are needed, you want to proceed carefully and thoughtfully. Policies are not written in a vacuum, and there will have been reasons behind every policy or procedure, as noted previously. To make a change, it is important first to understand the background.

Second, learn your library's process for changing policies and procedures. Who can propose a change and who can approve a change? If your change involves the strategic plan or the library's core values, it may require approval by the board of trustees or city council. If it is a simple procedure change, it may be able to be approved by the library's administration. In some cases, there will be a formal process for requesting a change. It could include several steps of approval. For example, a change in a circulation policy might need to be vetted first by the circulation staff, then by circulation supervisors or managers, then by library administration. No one appreciates an end run, so follow the library's guidelines.

Whoever the decision makers are, give them sufficient and appropriate background information. Here are some examples of the kinds of information that will be required to make a change:

- Why the change should be made: How will this change affect the library's service to teens and the relationship to the community?
- What impact the change will have on staffing: For example, show that after-school supervision will require fewer staff members if they don't have to spend time policing the "no-furniture-moving" rule.
- What impact the change will have on procedures: For example, school ID cards will be added to the list of acceptable identification for getting a library card.
- What impact the change will have on the budget: For example, will there be costs associated with changing signs or informational handouts?
- When the change will take effect: Will it require a rollout or pilot period, or can a date be set to make the change? Would it make sense to change the policy at the beginning of a fiscal year, calendar year, or school year?

Get teen input on the proposed changes and present it with your proposal. Showing that you have teen buy-in may go a long way toward making your point, especially if the change you are advocating appears to be more lenient than what currently exists.

Finally, be professional and composed at all times during the process. While the teen services librarian may be passionate about the need for a change that will empower teens, other library workers may see the change as threatening.

Using Data to Support Your Case

In looking at your teen services program, you may conclude, for example, that you could better serve the teens of the community with a larger collection. To do that, you will need not only more money to buy materials, but more space in the library to house the new materials. Where is the money, and for that matter, the space, going to come from?

Chances are it is going to have to come out of another department. For the sake of argument, let's say that you have concluded that the children's department is over-funded compared to the teen department, and you want to present the case that money should be transferred from children's to teen. How do you get there?

First, just because it is obvious to you doesn't mean it is obvious to everyone else (especially the children's department!), so start by looking at some of the input and output measures. It might be interesting to set side-by-side the following numbers:

- Teen materials budget and children's materials budget
- Teen materials budget as a percentage of the whole and children's materials budget as a percentage of the whole
- Number of teen staff per capita and number of children's staff per capita
- Percent of floor space designated for teens and percent of floor space designated for children
- Turnover rate of teen materials and turnover rate of children's materials

Because in almost every public library circulation of children's materials is far greater than that of teen materials, you may want to focus on percentages and per capita measures, rather than comparing straight numbers. But the point is to show that the teen area is understaffed and underfunded in comparison to the children's area. If you can support the case with evidence that the teen collection is used heavily, so much the better. Find out, for example, what percentage of the teen materials is checked out at any given moment. Show that when new materials are purchased, teen circulation goes up. Get input from teens about what they would like to see in the teen area.

All of this information will need to be presented to the decision makers, who may be a supervisor, a branch manager, a library director, or a library board. The information should be presented in ways that meet the needs of the audience. In Chapter 4 we will look at some ways of communicating the results of your evaluation.

Using Data to Plan for the Future

Keeping track of data works. It can be solid evidence that a department is thriving. At the Fairport (NY) Public Library, teen services librarian Stephanie Squicciarini keeps a simple list in Microsoft Word of the cumulative monthly circulation of young adult materials, along with the percentage of the whole library's circulation that the young adult (YA) collection represents. In the year before she was hired to be the first full-time teen librarian, the library circulated 12,259 YA items, or 2.1 percent of the library's circulation. Those numbers, both items and percentage, more than doubled at the end of her first year, and within six years, the library was circulating more YA materials in the first three months of the year than they had in the full year before she came on board. The percentage of YA circulation has grown to over 10 percent of the library's total circulation. Squicciarini says, "As overall library circ started dropping slightly, YA kept increasing and became a larger percentage of the overall circ. This has helped when fighting to maintain our YA budget and fight[ing] for more YA physical space. Hard to cut back on the only department to actually see an increase!" (Squicciarini, e-mail message to the author, October 12, 2011). Squicciarini also used these numbers in front of her library's board when the library was going out for a bond measure to build a new library. Certain members of the community were convinced that teens didn't read or use the library, but she was able to demonstrate to the board that they were wrong, and that the board was on the right track in advocating for teens and providing resources for them.

Charli Osborne, of the Oxford (MI) Public Library, had a similar success. She started with 180 square feet of space in an alcove, with two walls of shelving and no dedicated desk for teen services. She began collecting circulation statistics, and used them to order the types of materials that teens wanted. Soon her statistics justified the need for a teen materials budget separate from that of children's. She started doing programs for teens, and kept the statistics for those as well. When some space within the library that had been leased to another city department became available, she was ready with her numbers, and ended up with a teen space of twelve hundred square feet that included seven computers, a 10,000-item collection, and a service desk just for teens (Charli Osborne, e-mail message to the author, October 30, 2009).

You don't know when opportunities such as these may arise, so it is good to maintain a collection of statistics, no matter how basic. Even if you think there is no possibility that the library will ever be able to remodel, expand, or build a new building, you never know when a bequest or a grant might change the whole scene. If you are prepared with data to support the need for an expanded teen space or collection, you will be ahead of the game.

References

ALA (American Library Association). 2009. "Core Competences of Librarianship." American Library Association. http://www.ala.org/educationcareers/sites/ala.org.educationcareers/files/content/careers/corecomp/corecompetences/finalcorecompstat09.pdf.

TADL (Traverse Area District Library). 2003. "Policy 5.3: Access to Materials Based on Age." Traverse Area District Library. http://www.tadl.org/about/policies.

YALSA (Young Adult Library Services Association). 2010. "YALSA's Competencies for Librarians Serving Youth: Young Adults Deserve the Best." American Library Association. http://www.ala .org/yalsa/guidelines/yacompetencies2010.

4

Evaluation

Evaluation as a Decision-Making and Communication Tool

There is no point to doing evaluation for its own sake. Unless you know where you are going with an evaluation, the results will be ineffective and you will just be collecting pieces of paper. In evaluating a library's teen services program, it is critical first to decide what kinds of decisions might result from the evaluation. Following are some examples of decisions that might follow the evaluation:

- The library will dedicate more money to the teen collection.
- Teen services staff will receive more training.
- Policies will be rewritten to be more equitable to teen users.
- The library will find ways to increase teen usage of collections and services.
- The community's teens will have more opportunities to be of service.

None of these decisions can be made by any one individual. They all affect other departments of the library. They also have budget implications. There might also be more short-term decisions that result from evaluation of programs or services, such as decisions about the types of programs that work best for teens.

In all cases of evaluating teen programs and services, it is important to keep in mind the developmental needs of teens. Is the library, for example, offering teens support from nonparent adults? Is the library showing teens that adults in the community value youth? Are teens being given useful roles in planning and implementing programs and services and the opportunity to be of service? Are teens getting positive role models from adults and from other teens? Are they actively engaged in learning? Are they given the opportunity to take responsibility? These are all developmental assets from the Search Institute's list of "building blocks of healthy development" for adolescents and are all things that the library should consider in planning services (Search Institute, 2007).

Other questions to ask in looking at evaluating data are:

- Who needs to see this information? Who are the primary audiences? Does the information need to go to a supervisor, the library director, the library board, the community?

- What kinds of information do those different people need to see? How detailed must it be?
- What is the timeline for presenting the information? Is there a scheduled formal meeting where it should be presented, or can it be delivered casually, one-on-one?
- Do you have all the information that your audience is going to need or want?
- How are you going to report the information in a way that makes sense to the chosen audience?
- What costs are involved in collecting more information or in making changes?

The kind of report you give depends on the audience. People who are directly affected by the changes, like coworkers and supervisors, will need the most detailed report about any changes. These same people will be helpful in reviewing and commenting on any report before it is moved up the chain of command. They will also be most interested in any reports about existing activity, as it will either validate what they are doing or point to areas that need improvement. Managers and library directors will need to see how your evaluation fits into the bigger picture of the library. They will want to see how changes in teen services will affect the entire library and the library's relationship with the community. They will also be in tune with the political realities of the situation. Library board members, funders, and other outside stakeholders also want to see teen services as part of a larger community picture. They may want to see only the more positive results of your evaluation.

Give some consideration to the format of your presentation. In most cases, for a short presentation, simple charts or graphics will have much more impact than word- or number-intensive slides. Use some of the many online infographics tools to help you make your point. This need not be especially complicated. Angela Alcorn (2010), in her blog post "10 Awesome Free Tools to Make Infographics," writes, "Remember that it's all about quickly conveying the meaning behind complex data." So your infographic should be relatively self-explanatory.

For example, if you have collected comments on a survey or evaluation form, enter the comments into Wordle (http://www.wordle.net/) to create a word cloud that highlights the words or phrases that came up the most often. Figure 4.1 shows a Wordle word cloud that was created by entering the most frequently mentioned items when teens were asked what the ideal teen section of a library would include and what kinds of services they wanted.

If you want to share with the library board a brief summary of your summer reading program, consider using Microsoft PowerPoint or Publisher to make a poster demonstrating your results. Include a few statistics, such as the number of teens who registered and the number who met their reading goals, as well as something unexpected and interesting, such as "27 percent of teens at our gaming program were first-time library users." To make the poster eye-catching, include photos of teens.

Figure 4.1. Wordle Word Cloud

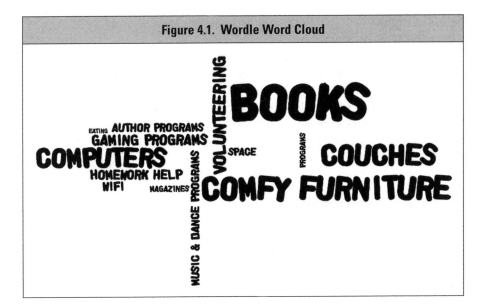

You can use stock photos from Microsoft Office's clip art library or get photos that are licensed for noncommercial use; better yet, use your own photos of teens at your programs and activities.

Even simple charts from Microsoft Excel can tell your story better than just plain numbers, no matter who your audience is. See some of the graphs and charts later in this chapter for examples. You can share your successes both formally and informally, orally and in written form. By knowing some specific details about your programs and services, you can share them when you meet coworkers in the break room, or run into a city councilor in the hallway. "Yes," you can say, "we had a great summer reading program. Twenty-seven percent of the teens who showed up for our gaming program were first-time library users! It was great to issue all those new cards, and show them all of the great things we offer at the library—they had no idea!"

If your library has a newsletter, e-newsletter, or Friends of the Library newsletter, you can use that venue to share successes about programs and services with the public. The community will not be interested in detailed statistics about programs, but it is a good opportunity to include some "feel-good" stories that will create a positive buzz for the library and for teen services. If your library issues an annual report, this is another chance to share some information about teen services. Many community members may think that teens do not use the library, and a few quick statistics about the number of teens who attend programs or the circulation of teen materials may be an eye-opener.

If you have an opportunity to talk with community groups, you might be able to go into a little more detail. These opportunities come up all the time, so if you have done the background work to collect the data and organize it, you will be prepared to insert a few pertinent items into the next report.

If your summer reading program or other programs are even partially grant funded, you will probably have to do a summary report at the end of the project. Funders are usually specific about the kinds of data that they want to see, and you should follow the grant instructions. Even if you do not receive a formal grant, but rather your Friends of the Library donate money for prizes, you should present them with a report about how the money was used. Knowing how many teens were served or hearing a report on program successes will encourage them to give again next year.

Outcome-Based Evaluation

As noted in Chapter 2, outcome-based evaluation is a way to measure the outcomes, or impacts, of service. It answers the question, "So what?" As Rhea Rubin says, "Teens are checking out more books? So what? What difference does it make to the young adults if they do or do not check out more books? What does it indicate about our aims?" (Rubin, 2006: 13). Outcomes should be specific and measurable and should indicate a specific impact on the user or participant. In short, outcomes tell the success stories of the library from the point of view of the library user, in this case teens. Outcomes generally measure benefits or changes for the user after participating in the program or activity. These are some types of changes that are typically measured:

- **Knowledge:** The participant learns something new, such as the fact that the library offers downloadable audiobooks, videos, and e-books.
- **Skills:** The participant acquires a new skill or hones a skill, such as using the library's databases, or playing a game.
- **Attitudes:** The participant's attitude changes; for example, a teen who thought the library had nothing to offer now sees the value in using the library's DVD collection.
- **Behavior:** The participant's behavior changes; for example, by participating in a homework assistance program, a teen begins to get homework assignments done on time.
- **Condition or status:** The participant's condition or status changes; e.g., a teen takes a GED workshop, passes the GED, and becomes a high school graduate.

Rubin suggests using an "if-then" chain to work either from what you want to do to the intended results, or from desired results back to potential services. For example, if the library wants to offer a summer reading program for teens, the chain might look like this:

- *If* the library offers a summer reading program for teens, *then* more teens will maintain their reading skills over the summer. *If* they maintain their reading skills, *then* they will get better grades in school. *If* they get better grades in school, *then* they will graduate from high school.

If, on the other hand, the starting goal is to improve the local high school graduation rate, the if-then statement might be this:

- *If* we want more students in our community to graduate from high school, *then* they need to get better grades in school. *If* we want them to get better grades in school, *then* they need good reading skills. *If* we offer a summer reading program, *then* more teens will maintain and improve their reading skills.

Measuring outcomes or impacts can be difficult and time-consuming. In the previous example, the outcomes are long term. To measure results effectively, you would need to know the current high school graduation rate and track it over several years. You would also need to follow individual participants in the summer reading program, to see if their grades improved and if they believed that their reading skills had improved after the summer reading program. However, outcomes make compelling stories and can certainly be worth the effort. More and more funders are insisting upon outcome-based evaluation as a condition of grants, so it is important to learn how to do it. You can start small, by doing simple pre- and post-program surveys. See the section on summer reading programs later in this chapter and Forms 6.2 and 6.3 in Chapter 6 for examples.

Another way to approach outcome-based evaluation would be to collaborate with a teacher or teachers, and focus on using summer reading to maintain or improve reading skills. The teacher could identify students whose reading skills were low or midrange, and the public library could focus on targeting those students for summer reading activities. In the fall, the teacher could evaluate the reading skills again to determine whether they had improved, maintained, or declined over the summer.

Evaluating YA Collections

In Chapter 3, we looked at some ways to use data to evaluate YA collections. Starting with local statistical data, you can get an overview of the size and age of a collection and how much it is used, at least in terms of checkouts. Another approach is to compare an individual collection with some of the composite numbers we looked at in Chapter 1. For example, the 2007 Public Library Data Service (PLDS) report had several comparison charts. Table 4.1 presents the PLDS comparison chart for circulation of young adult materials per young adult.

Let's assume that you work in a library with a service area population of 38,000 people, of whom 4,180 (11 percent) are teens, ages 12–18. In Table 4.1, we see that public libraries serving 25,000–49,999 people have an average (mean) circulation of 4.2 young adult items per young adult in the service area. The chart also shows that

Table 4.1. FY 2006 Circulation of Young Adult Materials per Young Adult							
Public Libraries Serving	Reporting Libraries	Mean or Average	High	Upper Quartile (75%)	Median (50%)	Lower Quartile (25%)	Low
1,000,000 and over	19	3.1	10.6	3.8	2.2	1.0	0.1
500,000 to 999,999	40	4.2	15.0	6.5	3.0	1.8	0.2
250,000 to 499,999	54	3.6	28.8	4.2	2.8	1.4	0.2
100,000 to 249,000	109	3.6	35.6	4.2	2.4	1.1	0.1
50,000 to 99,999	84	5.7	75.3	5.0	2.9	1.6	0.2
25,000 to 49,999	52	4.2	25.9	5.5	2.2	1.1	0.1
10,000 to 24,999	40	4.9	30.0	4.5	2.9	1.5	0.4
5,000 to 9,999	14	7.3	25.0	11.2	5.3	0.9	0.3
Under 5,000	5	6.1	20.4	$n < 11$	1.4	$n < 11$	0.6

$n < 11$ = less than 11 reporting

Source: Public Library Association. 2007. *Statistical Report 2007: Public Library Data Service, special section: Young Adult Services Survey.* Chicago: American Library Association.

numbers range from a high of 25.9 items per young adult to a low of 0.1 item per young adult, with a median of 2.2 items. So the first step is to see where your library fits in that continuum. This library had a yearly circulation of 58,148 items that were classified as teen materials. So the circulation per teen is 58,148 ÷ 4,180 = 13.9 items. Looking at the comparison chart, we see that this is well above the mean, and, indeed, in the upper quartile for libraries of our size. But suppose the circulation of teen items had been only 14,630. Then the circulation per item would be 14,630 ÷ 4,180 = 3.5 items. This is above the median, but below the mean, for libraries of the same size.

PLDS lists two other measures in summary form. Table 4.2 shows expenditures on young adult materials per young adult and Table 4.3 shows expenditures on young adult materials as a percentage of total materials expenditures. The expenditure per young adult is calculated by taking the young adult materials budget and dividing it by the number of teens in the service area. The expenditures as a percentage of the total are calculated by dividing the teen materials budget by the total materials budget. Let's assume we're still talking about our library with a service area population of 38,000 and a teen population of 4,180. We'll also say that the library's materials budget is $326,575. Our library spends $2.85 per teen for teen materials and that is 3.65 percent of the total materials budget. Looking in the column labeled "Public Libraries Serving" and the row "25,000 to 49,999" in Table 4.2, we see that the mean, or average, expenditure per young adult is $3.04, so our library lags on that measure. However, we are definitely in the chart's "upper quartile" (that is, greater than or equal to 75 percent of libraries surveyed) on this measure. Looking at Table 4.3, we see that the average of young adult materials expenditures as a percentage of the total is 4.0 percent, and our library is at 3.65 percent. In this case, we are not in the upper quartile, but we are above the median.

In addition to the summary charts, the PLDS report lists each library that responded to the survey. So you can also pick specific libraries to compare with your library. You should pick the libraries that seem most relevant to your purpose

Table 4.2. FY 2006 Young Adult Materials Expenditures per Young Adult (in dollars)							
Public Libraries Serving	Reporting Libraries	Mean or Average	High	Upper Quartile (75%)	Median (50%)	Lower Quartile (25%)	Low
1,000,000 and over	18	2.02	5.77	3.62	1.35	0.70	0.36
500,000 to 999,999	34	2.97	14.32	3.43	2.22	0.72	0.01
250,000 to 499,999	42	2.10	8.37	2.42	1.58	0.76	0.06
100,000 to 249,000	83	1.93	11.94	2.67	1.15	0.69	0.10
50,000 to 99,999	78	2.63	46.63	2.74	1.60	0.83	0.03
25,000 to 49,999	44	3.04	22.83	3.46	1.88	0.99	0.31
10,000 to 24,999	25	3.07	6.13	4.29	2.92	1.55	0.03
5,000 to 9,999	9	3.22	5.73	$n < 11$	3.20	$n < 11$	0.25
Under 5,000	1	5.78	5.78	$n < 11$	$n < 3$	$n < 11$	5.78

$n < 11$ = less than 11 reporting

Source: Public Library Association. 2007. *Statistical Report 2007: Public Library Data Service, special section: Young Adult Services Survey*. Chicago: American Library Association.

Table 4.3. FY 2006 Young Adult Materials Expenditures as Percentage of Total Materials Expenditures							
Public Libraries Serving	Reporting Libraries	Mean or Average	High	Upper Quartile (75%)	Median (50%)	Lower Quartile (25%)	Low
1,000,000 and over	18	5.2	13.9	9.1	3.8	2.3	0.9
500,000 to 999,999	40	4.3	18.4	6.0	3.5	1.7	0.1
250,000 to 499,999	45	3.6	11.9	4.5	3.5	2.2	0.3
100,000 to 249,000	96	4.6	66.4	4.7	3.0	1.9	0.2
50,000 to 99,999	90	3.5	20.8	4.6	2.8	1.7	0.2
25,000 to 49,999	50	4.0	14.6	4.9	3.2	2.0	0.2
10,000 to 24,999	33	4.8	11.3	6.3	4.6	2.8	0.8
5,000 to 9,999	14	6.3	12.5	10.1	6.8	2.5	0.3
Under 5,000	1	10.4	10.4	$n < 11$	$n < 3$	$n < 11$	10.4

$n < 11$ = less than 11 reporting

Source: Public Library Association. 2007. *Statistical Report 2007: Public Library Data Service, special section: Young Adult Services Survey*. Chicago: American Library Association.

and audience. You may want to concentrate on other libraries of approximately the same size as yours. Since the report lists actual population figures, you can choose the five or six libraries that are closest in size to your own. Those libraries may not be the most relevant to your situation, however, depending on how they are funded, where they are located, and other factors. So you might pick out the libraries that are in your state or region, or the libraries whose overall materials budget is similar to yours. Table 4.4 shows six libraries, ours (Happy Hollow) and five libraries of similar size. In this comparison, we are close to the middle of the pack, showing a higher expenditure per teen than three other libraries, and lower than two, although clearly in the top tier. As a percentage of the total materials expenditure, our young adult materials expenditure is right in the middle. But the libraries considered have a wide range of materials money available: Pleasant Hill spends only $165,488 per year on materials, while Pleasanton spends $406,081.

Table 4.4. YA Materials Expenditure per YA (Comparable-Sized Libraries)						
			YA Materials Expenditure			
Library	Population of Service Area	YA Population	Current Fiscal Year ($)	Per YA ($)	YA % of Total	Total Library Materials Exp. ($)
Pleasantville	39,824	4,000	3,974	0.99	2.21	179,819.00
Pleasant Valley	39,548	4,000	1,500	0.38	0.99	151,515.15
Pleasanton	38,658	5,026	15,959	3.18	3.93	406,081.42
Happy Hollow	**38,000**	**4,180**	**11,920**	**2.85**	**3.65**	**326,575.34**
Pleasant Hill	37,475	2,998	12,544	4.18	7.58	165,488.13
Pleasant Falls	37,132	5,600	10,000	1.79	5.58	179,211.47

So, as a reality check, we compare our expenditures on young adult materials to libraries with a similar materials budget. In Table 4.5, we see that libraries with a similar materials budget vary in size from a population of 35,632 for Springville to 70,097 for Spring Valley. Expenditures on young adult materials per young adult vary from less than a dollar to almost five dollars, while the percentage of the total materials budget ranges from 1–8 percent. Again, in this scenario, our library (Happy Hollow) is somewhere in the middle.

So what? That depends on your particular situation. If you want to prove that you are right where you should be, these numbers might be sufficient. If, on the other hand, your library director is extremely competitive with the neighboring Pleasant

Table 4.5. YA Materials Expenditure (Comparable-Sized Budgets)						
			YA Materials Expenditure			
Library	Population of Service Area	YA Population	Current Fiscal Year ($)	Per YA ($)	YA % of Total	Total Library Materials Exp. ($)
Springville	35,632	1,928	7,500	3.89	2.40	312,382.00
Spring Valley	70,097	6,309	31,177	4.94	8.00	389,724.00
Springtown	54,834	4,387	4,000	0.91	1.05	380,103.00
Happy Hollow	**38,000**	**4,180**	**11,920**	**2.85**	**3.65**	**326,575.34**
Spring Hill	67,112	6,711	8,100	1.21	2.34	346,040.00
Spring Falls	65,020	7,152	18,055	2.52	5.01	360,065.00

Hill Library, you might want to show her that even though Pleasant Hill has a smaller budget, they spend a greater amount on young adult materials—the dollar amount, the per-young adult figure, and the percentage of the total all show us this.

Another way to use these numbers is to compare the expenditures per teen and percentage of the budget spent on teen materials to the expenditures per child, and the budget spent on children's materials. In Table 4.6 we use the same libraries as in the previous example, and we add in information about their expenditures on children's materials. We can see that all of the libraries spend considerably more on children's materials than they do on young adult materials: in dollar amount, in per capita amount, and in percentage of the total. To illustrate the numbers graphically, Figure 4.2 shows the expenditures per capita in a comparison graph. But that does not necessarily mean that teens are being treated unjustly in any of these situations. This is a good example of an instance where you need to know the big picture. For one

Table 4.6. Children's/YA Materials Comparison					
			YA Materials Expenditure		
Library	**Population of Service Area**	**YA Pop.**	**Current Fiscal Year ($)**	**Per YA ($)**	**YA % of Total**
Springville	35,632	1,928	7,500	3.89	2.40
Spring Valley	70,097	6,309	31,177	4.94	8.00
Springtown	54,834	4,387	4,000	0.91	1.05
Happy Hollow	**38,000**	**4,180**	**11,920**	**2.85**	**3.65**
Spring Hill	67,112	6,711	8,100	1.21	2.34
Spring Falls	65,020	7,152	18,055	2.52	5.01
(Columns continued below)					
			Children's Materials Expenditure		
Library	**Total Library Materials Exp. ($)**	**Child Pop.**	**Current Fiscal Year ($)**	**Per Child ($)**	**Child % of Total**
Springville	312,382.00	6,928	53,000	7.65	16.97
Spring Valley	389,724.00	14,284	110,564	7.74	28.37
Springtown	380,103.00	7,930	96,541	12.17	25.40
Happy Hollow	**326,575.34**	**8,360**	**114,301**	**13.67**	**35.00**
Spring Hill	346,040.00	10,782	32,710	3.03	9.45
Spring Falls	360,065.00	13,152	75,113	5.71	20.86

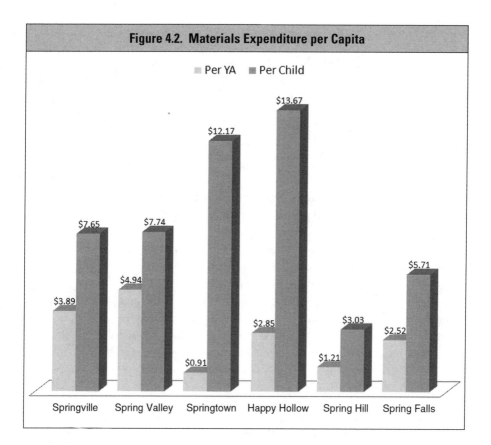

Figure 4.2. Materials Expenditure per Capita

thing, look at the population numbers. In most of these libraries, there are two or three times as many children as teens. Plus, as we saw in Chapter 3, teens use materials from all parts of the library. In the example we used there, only about a third of the materials checked out by teens were from the teen collection. So expenditures per teen are actually much higher than they appear at first glance, since money that is nominally going to buy adult or children's materials is in fact buying materials that teens are using. But depending on your audience and your goals, these are good numbers to know.

One way to look at a collection is to compare the use of different parts of the collection. This is called relative use, which is the idea that "in a patron-driven collection, a subject area that has 15 percent of the collection's volumes should have about 15 percent of the use.... Any area in which the percentage of use is higher than its percentage of the collection should be supported with more items" (Greiner and Cooper, 2007: 118). So, for example, in Table 4.7, or graphically in Figure 4.3, we see that in the sample library, 55 percent of the collection is adult materials, 37 percent is children's materials, and 8 percent is teen materials. By calculating the percent of

Table 4.7. Relative Use by Age

	Collection Size	% of Collection	Circulation	% of Circulation
Adult	53,801	55	31,555	47
Children's	36,122	37	29,787	44
Teen	7,414	8	5,699	9
Total	97,337	100	67,041	100

circulation in each of those areas, we see that adult is 47 percent of circulation, children's is 44 percent, and teen is 9 percent. So both teen and children's have a higher percentage of use than of the collection.

The same relative use calculation can be made within a collection. For example, in the teen collection, you could calculate relative use on the different types of materials, as in Table 4.8. In this collection, the areas where percentage of use is higher than percentage of the collection are graphic novels, music CDs, and DVDs. This does not necessarily mean that the library needs to go out and buy more items in those classifications, but it is something to consider as you evaluate the collection. It might also be an indication that parts of the collection need weeding. If the print collection is weeded heavily, leaving mainly the newer items that circulate more, the relative use will shift over time.

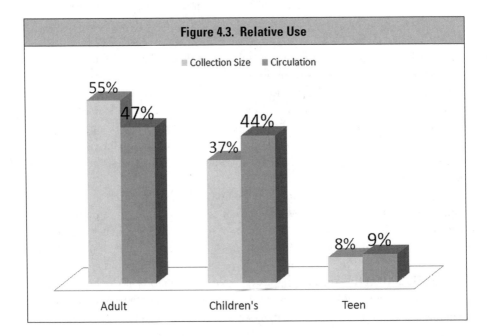

Figure 4.3. Relative Use

Table 4.8. Relative Use of Teen Collection				
	Number of Items	Yearly Circulation	% of Collection	% of Circulation
Teen Fiction	1,720	12,054	16	18
Teen Science Fiction	482	2,316	5	3
Teen Paperbacks	2,941	14,734	28	22
Teen Mystery	38	94	0	0
Teen Short Stories	36	130	0	0
Total Teen Fiction	**5,217**	**29,328**	**50**	**43**
Teen Nonfiction	1,561	3,170	15	5
Teen Graphic Novels	1,855	16,154	18	24
Teen Audiobooks	322	1,318	3	2
Teen Music CDs	1,423	16,168	14	24
Teen DVDs	153	1,702	1	3
Total	**10,531**	**67,840**	100	100

Evaluating Teen Summer Reading Programs

Evaluation for summer reading programs has typically consisted of some basic statistical measures:

- Number of teens who signed up
- Number of teens who met their goals (books read, pages read, hours spent reading, etc.)
- Number of programs offered
- Number of teens who attended programs

All of these are useful enough measures, especially when compared over multiple years. Calculating completion rates (number of teens who met their goals or completed the program divided by total number of teens who signed up) can give you an idea about the engagement of teens, especially over time. Likewise, calculating the number of teens who signed up as a percentage of the number of teens in your service area will give you an idea of how well you are reaching into the community.

However, teens, even more than children, have many things competing for their time during the summer. A successful summer reading program for teens might include elements outside of the normal statistical counts. For example, you could do a quick survey when teens sign up for the summer reading program. Ask two or three simple questions, such as:

- How many hours per week do you read for pleasure?
- How much do you enjoy reading? (not at all, a little, some, a lot, very much)
- How well do you feel you understand what you read?

Then ask the same questions after they have completed the program to determine if there has been any change: do they report more hours of reading, more enjoyment, greater comprehension? See Chapter 6 for some sample surveys.

Doing pre- and post-surveys can also enable you to perform some outcome-based evaluation of your summer reading program. Your goal, for example, might be that 75 percent of participants increased their reading enjoyment as a result of the summer reading program. You can get some of the information from the surveys, but you might also want to include individual interviews or informal discussions to get an even better feel for whether they now enjoy reading more than they did before.

Ask teens to evaluate the success of the summer reading program. Give them an opportunity to let you know what works and what doesn't work for them, what they would keep, and what they would discard or improve. If you offer prizes for completion of goals, ask their opinions of the prizes. What kinds of prizes would be more appealing to them? Would they rather have certificates that waive library fines, gift cards for a local bookstore/music store/fast-food restaurant, or something concrete such as a flash drive or tote bag? Would they like to have hours spent reading count toward dollars to buy an animal for the Heifer Project (http://www.heifer.org/)?

Many libraries that participate in their statewide summer reading programs must submit a formal report at the end of the summer. Often submitted by the library director or youth services manager, this may include data on both children's and teen summer reading programs. Whether or not you are required to submit a summary to a funder or supervisor, keeping track of your successes and failures can help you plan for the next year. Chapter 6 provides a sample final report for a summer reading program that calls for a narrative report, including anecdotes, as well as a quantitative report that asks for information not only about participants but also about publicity and marketing.

Part of evaluating the program is to look at it from the point of view of the library, and this longer summary report includes such information. How much did the program cost—in dollars, in staff time, and in donated time and materials? In calculating staff time, you need to include not just the time spent at the various events but also staff time involved in signing up participants, reviewing reading logs, doing publicity and marketing, seeking out performers, lining up volunteers, collecting prizes, and anything else that was related to the summer reading program. At the end of the summer, comparing teen responses to the program to the time, energy, and dollars put in by the library will help you determine whether the program was an overall success, and what changes you might want to make for the future.

Evaluating Teen Programs and Special Events

Evaluating library programs and events is a way to answer some questions about what you are doing and how you are succeeding. Start by asking some basic questions:

- Whom do you want to serve by this program?
  - Whom did you market it to?
  - How did you market it?
  - Who actually attended?
- What do you want them to get out of the program?
  - To learn a skill
  - To have fun in the library
  - To be introduced to new technologies or materials
  - To meet like-minded teens
  - To have an opportunity to share their skills with others
  - To learn that the library and community value their interests
- What do you (the library) want to get out of the program?
  - Bring in new library users
  - Raise library visibility
  - Increase circulation
  - Recruit teens for an advisory board
  - Have a positive public relations event
  - Build community partnerships
  - Market library materials, services, and programs
- How will you know if you have been successful?
  - Pre- and post-program surveys
  - User satisfaction survey
  - Staff survey or observation
  - Attendee comments
  - Attendance count

The type of evaluation you do will depend on what you want to learn as well as on the audience for your evaluation. Will it need to be presented to a supervisor, the library director, or the library board?

Informal Evaluations

One of the simplest forms of tracking for programs is to count attendance. For even more information, note the sex of attendees and their age or grade. Count attendees in the target age group, but also count attendees and spectators in other age groups. Often younger children come to teen programs, and parents come as spectators or participants.

Another way to track numbers is to require preregistration for an event. Interestingly, requiring registration can also serve the purpose of building up some buzz and ensuring that the attendees actually show up on the day. Having a count of preregistered attendees will give you an idea of the amount of supplies or seats that you need for the program.

If you are having a "drop-in" program, such as a craft program or a gaming program, it can be very useful to count attendees throughout the program. Do a head count every 15 or 20 minutes to get an idea of the flow of the program. This will also enable you to learn which elements of the program were the most popular. Another way to capture this information is to use photographs. Taking pictures throughout the program will show you the numbers of attendees at different points throughout the program and also allow you to note the reactions of the attendees. Photos can later be used for marketing future programs or for presenting documentation on the success of the program to the library director, board, or other stakeholders. If you plan to use the photos other than internally, be sure to follow your library's policy on photographing or videotaping members of the public and get releases when required. Now that so many teens have phones with camera capabilities, you can invite them to submit their photos of the event, which can also be used in publicity and evaluation.

Comments of attendees during and immediately after a program can be a valuable source of information. Listen to the teens and make notes of what they are saying, or capture them on a voice or video recorder. Ask an open question or two, if needed, such as "What would you like us to do next time we have an event like this?" or "What was your favorite part of today's program?"

In the days after a program, ask the teens you see both inside and outside the library whether or not they attended. If they did, ask what they thought of the program. If they didn't, ask why not. Keep a record of these informal evaluations by making notes. One technique is to keep a document into which you simply continue to type in comments you hear from the teens and others. You may also find that occasionally a teen or a parent or other library user will leave you a note or send you an e-mail commenting on your programs or thanking you for something that you have done. These are great informal evaluations. If you keep them, they can be shared with a supervisor at the time of formal staff evaluations. It is also just fun to read them sometimes when you are feeling discouraged.

Formal Evaluations

Formal evaluations for programs and events are usually done with evaluation forms that are handed to participants and filled out on the spot. It's easy to whip up an evaluation form, but a little more difficult to create one that gives you the information you want and need. Think about what it is that you want to learn from the evaluation before you create a form. And don't ask if you are not prepared to take action. Of course, you are not going to be able to do everything that everyone suggests, but you should be prepared to take some kind of action based on the responses to your questions.

If you expect users, especially teens, to give you honest feedback, you need to keep the form brief and to the point. This may mean that you can't ask everything every time. You may want to concentrate, for example, on finding out what the most effective form of publicity is for your programs. In this case, the bulk of your questions should be focused on where they heard about the program and what convinced them to come.

The simplest kinds of questions are ones with a limited set of answers. For example, ask your respondents to rank a program from 1 (poor) to 5 (excellent). But often you will want to ask open-ended questions about your programs and solicit comments from the participants. Reading comments can seem overwhelming and the information can often seem contradictory. But it is possible to analyze and organize comments in a way that will be useful to your evaluation. Try these steps:

- Read all of the comments one time through.
- The second time through, start to organize comments into broad categories such as complaints, praise, suggestions.
- Within those categories, break comments down further into subcategories by topic (complaints about programs, complaints about staff, complaints about food).
- Look for patterns or associations in the categories.
- Note where there are "outliers"—where only one person had a complaint about a program, for example, while everyone else praised it.

You can then create a summary document that synthesizes the comments and focuses on the lessons learned. For example, "The vast majority of the comments about the summer reading program were positive, although there was general agreement that there was not enough food supplied for the end-of-summer party." Or "When asked what types of programs they would like to have in the future, the most common response was gaming programs, followed by art programs and author programs."

There are various free online tools you can use to create surveys, including Survey Monkey (http://www.surveymonkey.com/), Zoomerang (http://www.zoomerang.com/), and Kwik Surveys (http://www.kwiksurveys.com/). Online surveys make it easy to compile results, and they may appeal to some teens, but the trick is getting them to actually sit down and fill out the survey. Paper surveys have the advantage of instant response but are more labor-intensive for the compiler. Especially if you are doing a large survey, like a needs assessment or other survey to get teens to evaluate your overall teen services program, you might want to do a combination of online and paper surveys, giving teens the opportunity to respond in their preferred manner.

Distributing survey forms or links outside of the library will help to ensure that you get at least some responses from non–library users. One way to encourage participation in this type of survey is to have a prize drawing for participants. If your library or Friends of the Library can donate a few gift cards or small electronics, this can be a real incentive for teens to complete the survey. If you do not want to connect individual names with survey responses, a note at the end of the survey can instruct them to submit their names via e-mail or at a library service desk.

Chapter 6 contains some sample evaluation forms for programs and events.

Focus Groups

Another way to get information about programs and services is to do focus groups. Gathering a group of teens together and asking them to share their perceptions and opinions can give you a lot of information, but you do want to go into the process fully prepared.

- Plan for about an hour to an hour and a half.
- Invite six to ten teens to attend, get a commitment from them, and follow up with reminders before the date. There will always be some who don't show up, so you might want to invite more rather than fewer participants.
- Decide specifically what it is you want to learn (e.g., whether a new program idea you have will work, what kinds of activities they would be interested in joining, how a new facility would best meet their needs).
- Prepare five or six open-ended questions ahead of time.
- Bring food!
- Set some ground rules: everyone's ideas are good, respond specifically to the questions, don't talk over others, and so forth.
- Record the session, either with an audio or video recorder, or by having an assistant take notes.

During the focus group, be friendly but maintain control by keeping the participants focused on the question you are asking. Move them along to the next question when everyone has had a chance to respond. Encourage responses through nodding and eye contact, but don't shut down the conversation by showing a strong reaction to anything that is said.

As with comments from survey forms, you will need to analyze and organize the comments from a focus group after the session. Note which responses came up the most, which got general agreement from the participants, and which were just one person's opinion. Compile a summary.

Evaluating Staff

Evaluating library staff is ultimately the job of supervisors and managers, but in looking at a library's teen services and programs, staff competence, knowledge, skills, and attitudes will make a difference in how effectively those services and programs are delivered. So any evaluation of teen services and programs needs to take a look at who is delivering those services and programs, with an eye to providing the training and support necessary for staff to offer the best possible service to teens.

All library staff should have a basic knowledge of adolescent development, but especially staff who are designated to serve teens. They should be familiar with information such as that discussed in Chapter 1 about teen brain development and the developmental tasks that adolescents face. In addition, this knowledge of teens should extend to a knowledge of teen literature and of popular culture and the kinds of technologies that teens use.

Again, all library reference staff, but especially those working directly with teens, should have basic knowledge about how to perform an effective reference interview and also some training in dealing with homework assignments (imposed queries) as well as the kinds of popular culture and personal queries that teens bring to the reference desk.

The fundamentals of the organization of information and of communication and marketing are other areas in which public services staff should be fluent. Librarians and library workers who are assigned specifically to serve teens must be aware of selection tools beyond the basic ones used in collection development for adults and children. Sources of reviews and information about graphic novels, anime, paperback series, magazines, and other types of popular culture materials will need to be added to the knowledge base of the teen-serving librarian.

Finally, library staff who work with teens need to have the ability to communicate effectively with them. They need to be able to engage teens in the work of the library, tapping into the energy, enthusiasm, and skills that teens bring to all that they do. And they need to be able to remain friendly yet firm in dealing with teen behavior in the library.

One way to evaluate staff in these areas is to use "YALSA's Competencies for Serving Youth: Young Adults Deserve the Best" (YALSA, 2010). In Chapter 5, we will look in more detail at ways to use the competencies with staff, and the competencies themselves are listed in Chapter 6. In general, however, the competencies can serve as a template for developing training plans for all library workers who interact with teens. In Chapter 6, you will find a sample self-assessment tool that is based on the competencies. Using this tool, or something like it, is one way to determine which topics a particular staff member needs more training on. Supervisors could use the competencies or items from the self-assessment to identify a few areas to include in the goals for young adult librarians when doing their performance evaluations.

To find out how teens and other library users perceive the knowledge, skills, and attitudes of the staff, you could include a question or two about staff interactions in other evaluation forms. For a more complete picture, try a survey or focus group in which you ask specific questions about how teens regard their contacts with library staff—both teen services staff and other library staff. Chapter 6 includes a sample satisfaction survey.

In general, in evaluating staff interactions with teens, you want to know several key indicators:

- How responsive are staff members? Do they anticipate the needs of teens? Do they ask if they can help, or wait to be asked? Do they treat all questions in a respectful, unbiased manner?
- How courteous are staff members? Are they approachable and welcoming? Do they talk directly to teens? Do they demonstrate search techniques and offer to teach?
- How well do staff members perform? Do they understand the questions being asked, and get clarification? Do they follow up? Do they treat teens respectfully and confidentially? Do they know the library's collection and resources?
- How reliable are staff members? Is the information and guidance they provide accurate? Are they available when needed? Does the information they provide meet the needs of the teen user (e.g., not too much, but not too little)? Is the information they provide current?
- How satisfied are the teens? Do they get the materials they need? Do they feel empowered to find information on their own? Do they feel that they are treated fairly? Are they willing to return? Are they willing to recommend the library to their friends?

References

Alcorn, Angela. 2010. "10 Awesome Free Tools to Make Infographics." *MakeUseOf* (blog), October 8. http://www.makeuseof.com/tag/awesome-free-tools-infographics.

Greiner, Tony, and Bob Cooper. 2007. *Analyzing Library Collection Use with Excel*. Chicago: American Library Association.

Rubin, Rhea Joyce, for the Public Library Association. 2006. *Demonstrating Results: Using Outcome Measurement in Your Library*. Chicago: American Library Association.

Search Institute. 2007. "40 Developmental Assets® for Adolescents (ages 12–18)." http://www.search-institute.org/content/40-developmental-assets-adolescents-ages-12-18.

YALSA (Young Adult Library Services Association). 2010. "YALSA's Competencies for Librarians Serving Youth: Young Adults Deserve the Best." American Library Association. http://www.ala.org/yalsa/guidelines/yacompetencies2010.

5
Best Practices

What an Excellent Teen Services Program Looks Like

Libraries vary widely in size, capacity, budget, population, demographics, and location, so it is impossible to say that there is any one perfect model for an excellent teen services program. What works in one library may not work in another. Still, there are some characteristics that seem to be common to excellence in teen services. An excellent teen services program involves and engages the teens in the community, treats them respectfully, and values their contributions to the community and the library. An excellent teen services program meets at least some of the developmental needs of teens and offers materials, services, and programs that teens want. An excellent teen services program should be an integral part of the library and the community at large.

In an ideal envisioned future, every library would have staff who are dedicated to serving teens and who are trained in adolescent development and knowledgeable about the materials and services that teens want and need. There would be a dedicated space for teens in the library, but teens would be welcome in all parts of the library and treated respectfully by all library staff and by the whole community.

Getting to this ideal future is the ultimate goal of evaluating a library's teen programs and services. Fortunately, there are tools to help, and here we will focus on the YALSA Competencies and the Public Library Evaluation Tool. The competencies are geared more toward individual teen services librarians, and the evaluation tool is focused on a library's overall commitment to service to teens. The competencies and the evaluation tool can be found in Chapter 6, and on the YALSA website at http://www.ala.org/yalsa/guidelines.

Using the YALSA Competencies

Competencies are skills, behaviors, or knowledge that are identified as being integral to the performance of a particular type of work. There are different sets of competencies for librarians and library workers, depending on the setting and emphasis. The American Library Association identifies "The Core Competences of Librarianship . . . [that]

define the knowledge to be possessed by all persons graduating from ALA-accredited master's programs in library and information studies" (ALA, 2009). YALSA has developed a set of competencies for librarians who serve young adults, ages 12–18. As the introduction to the competencies states, "Individuals who demonstrate the knowledge and skills laid out in this document will be able to provide quality library service for and with teenagers" (YALSA, 2010). Competencies are not intended to judge individuals, but rather to provide a framework within which individuals and libraries can evaluate and improve their service to teenagers. See Chapter 6 for the full list of YALSA competencies.

The YALSA competencies were created as a means to help libraries improve their overall service and increase their public value to the community. They were first written in 1981 and have been revised several times over the years to keep up with the latest research and trends, and especially to incorporate the principles of positive youth development. As with other lists of competencies, these can be used as a framework for staff training, as a basis for writing job descriptions for teen services librarians, and as guiding principles for speaking out about the importance of teen services in libraries and the role that a good teen services program can play in creating a stronger, better-integrated community.

The competencies are divided into seven different areas of concentration, although there are plenty of common themes throughout. The first area is Leadership and Professionalism, both of which are key to providing the best possible service to teens. Often, especially in public libraries, service for teens is a low priority. Many librarians, library workers, and members of the public find teens to be difficult to work with, and a little scary, and so their tendency is to ignore them or hope they go away. Or perhaps teens are seen as just slightly older children or slightly younger adults, and therefore services specifically designated for them are not seen as necessary, but rather a frill.

The competencies in the area of leadership and professionalism are geared to helping teen-serving librarians present themselves in such a way that they can make the needs of teens heard and understood in the library and in the community. By assuming leadership to identify the needs of young adults and advocate for service excellence, by having and demonstrating a commitment to professionalism and ethical behavior, and by taking an active role in their own professional growth and career development, librarians can ultimately better serve teens and the community. By helping teens become lifelong library users, by involving teens in the services they receive, and by modeling a commitment to building assets in youth, librarians can have a positive impact on the development of healthy, successful young adults. And finally, librarians can serve teens by taking a leadership role in training other library staff in the best practices of working with teens.

The second area of the competencies is Knowledge of Client Group. Knowing who teens are, understanding their developmental needs, recognizing and keeping up with their interests, and having an understanding and respect for diverse values—cultural, religious, and ethnic—and special needs of all types will help the teen-serving librarian better explain teens to the rest of the world.

The third competency area is Communication, Marketing, and Outreach. This area is mostly about serving teens well by building and maintaining relationships not only with teens, but with others, including library or school staff, supervisors, community leaders, other youth-serving professionals, and the community at large. It's about advocating for teens at all levels.

The fourth competency area is Administration, which is about keeping the teen department healthy by doing all the kinds of things that administrators do—strategic planning, community analysis and needs assessment, budgeting, planning facilities, professional development, and documentation—and including teens in these activities. Often a YA librarian is essentially a department of one. There may be no one else in the library whose job it is to focus on doing these types of administrative tasks for the teen services area. By learning these skills, the librarian is not only improving service for teens but also preparing himself or herself to be a supervisor one day.

The fifth competency area is Knowledge of Materials. This focuses on the need for teen-serving librarians to maintain appropriate collections that meet the informational and recreational needs of teens, and to serve as a resource for the library, teens, and the community in the area of young adult materials in all kinds of formats.

The sixth competency area is Access to Information. This includes physical access, including organization and display of materials. It also includes intellectual access, including helping teens learn how to access and evaluate information independently, and ensuring that they have access to the full range of materials and resources that the library has to offer.

The seventh competency area is Services. This covers not only programs, but all aspects of teen services: collections, reference, readers' advisory, outreach, and physical and virtual spaces.

There are different ways to use the competencies to evaluate a teen services program or librarian. Very few individuals will have all of the knowledge and skills listed at the highest level. Competencies by their very nature are goals to aim for and grow into. Here are some suggestions for using the competencies:

- The librarian and his or her supervisor sit down with the competencies and go through them one by one, discussing areas in which the librarian is already proficient, and areas in which he or she could use training and/or improvement. They set priorities, and these become part of the librarian's yearly performance goals.
- The librarian uses the competencies, along with *Young Adults Deserve the Best: YALSA's Competencies in Action* (Flowers, 2011) to develop a plan of action for training. He or she presents these to the supervisor with a request for specific training opportunities or with specific plans for change and improvement in the

teen services department. Chapter 6 includes a self-assessment tool that was taken primarily from the competencies that could be used to start this process.

- A library director or manager uses the competencies to determine where the gaps are in library staff education and training. As a result of this analysis, he or she updates job descriptions or professional development plans or makes changes in policies or procedures.

Using the YALSA Teen Services Evaluation Tool

YALSA's Teen Services Evaluation Tool was created by a task force of YALSA members in 2010, at the direction of YALSA's board of directors. The intention was to create a rubric to evaluate a public library's overall level of success in providing services to teens. As the introduction to the tool states:

> Potential users of this tool include library administrators, library trustees, teen services librarians, and community members and job-seekers hoping to assess a library's commitment to teen services. The tool is not intended to be an evaluation of an individual teen services librarian, but rather of an institution's program; however, of necessity some things will apply specifically to teen services staff. The areas for evaluation are derived primarily from YALSA's "Competencies for Librarians Serving Youth: Young Adults Deserve the Best." Not every element of the rubric will apply to every library situation, but the tool can serve as a place to begin the conversation about what constitutes excellent public library service for teens. (YALSA, 2010)

The tool is divided into the seven competency areas, and within those areas, specific essential elements are listed. (See Chapter 6 for the complete evaluation tool.) For each element, the tool defines library services on a continuum from "Distinguished" to "Below Basic." Also for each element, the tool includes examples and further resources to supplement the element.

How Library Administrators Can Use the Evaluation Tool

To use the evaluation tool internally, the first step would be for the library administrator to honestly assess the library's place on the continuum in each of the essential elements. The next step would be to determine the areas in which the library could improve its services. Depending on the areas involved, this might involve training staff, allocating or reallocating resources, rewriting policies or procedures, or other activities. The administrator could also use the tool to acknowledge the successes that the library has already achieved in providing high-quality services for teens. If you start by saying to staff, "Here are the areas in which we are distinguished," it is much easier to continue on with, "Now, let's see what we can do to move these other areas from 'basic' to 'proficient.'"

Using the tool externally can work in much the same way. Administrators can share successes with library boards, local and municipal governing bodies, and the community at large, while also bolstering the case for the need to modify budgets, strategic plans, or policies. Or, for example, a library director could take one section of the tool each month for seven months, and spend five minutes of each meeting of the board of trustees demonstrating where the library fit in each element, and what plans, if any, there are to improve.

See, for example, Table 5.1, which shows just the first two elements of the Leadership and Professionalism section. The director highlights where she believes the library falls on the continuum and then adds a column at the end to describe her plans for change and improvement. These items, then, become part of the director's goals for the coming year: to examine the library's statistics to determine whether teen services are receiving an equitable and proportionate amount of resources, and then to make next year's budget request accordingly. At the same time, presenting the evaluation matrix allows her to show the trustees that, overall, the library is doing fairly well, falling, for example, in the "Proficient" column for most items, in the "Distinguished" and "Basic" areas for a few, and never in "Below Basic."

How Trustees and Governing Bodies Can Use the Evaluation Tool

Library boards of trustees can use the evaluation tool proactively to assess how their libraries are succeeding at providing excellent service to teens. There are likely to be many areas on the matrix that trustees will not have personal knowledge about. And, in most cases, the level of detail provided in the tool is far beyond what a trustee would need to know. However, the tool could enable trustees to ask appropriate questions when the library presents them with budgets, policies, and strategic plans. So, for example, when the library director presents the budget for approval, a trustee might ask whether there is a line item for teen materials, and what the staff levels are for teen services, as compared with children's and adult services. Or, when a library is undertaking a community needs assessment, the trustee's role would be to ensure that teen input was solicited and used.

Knowing where the library fits on the continuum provided by the tool can also give trustees valuable information that they can share when they are in the community, talking about the value the library provides. Knowing, for example, that teens are "encouraged to use their skills in creating and implementing programs and services, volunteering, and applying for employment in the library" (YALSA, 2011: Section 4f) is useful when talking to outsiders who think that teens never go to the library, or only use it to hang out on the computers.

A trustee who is genuinely interested in teen services might find it useful to make an appointment with the library director (perhaps also including a teen services

Table 5.1. Plan for Change			
Leadership and Professionalism			
Essential Element	**Distinguished**	**Proficient**	**Basic**
Equitable funding and staffing levels	Library maintains line items in the budget for YA materials and staff at levels proportionate to YA usage and circulation.	Line item for YA materials budget; at least one librarian FTE devoted to YA services for each branch.	**Line item for YA materials budget. Some staff (professional or paraprofessional) devoted to YA services.**
Commitment to professionalism and ethical behavior	All library staff demonstrate extensive knowledge of ALA Code of Ethics, ALA Bill of Rights, YALSA Competencies and Guidelines for Service to Teens. The library defends YA services and the rights of teens to privacy and access. YA staff are actively involved in at least one professional organization on the national, regional, state, or local level. Subscriptions to appropriate professional journals are provided by library and accessible to all interested staff.	**YA staff demonstrate knowledge of ALA Code of Ethics, ALA Bill of Rights, and YALSA Competencies and Guidelines for Service to Teens; defend YA services and the rights of teens to privacy and access. YA staff belong to a professional organization and read appropriate professional journals.**	YA staff read appropriate professional journals.

(Columns continued on facing page)

librarian in the meeting) to go over the entire tool and get input into what the library is doing and how it might improve. This would be an opportunity to get to a greater level of detail than would be appropriate at a normal meeting of the board. It might turn out, for example, that while the library does not technically have a separate teen materials budget line item, they do in fact track spending on teen materials, and that the amount spent each year matches teen usage and circulation, compared to that of other parts of the library.

How Library Patrons and Community Members Can Use the Evaluation Tool

As with library trustees, the level of detail in the evaluation tool may be more than most library users and community members will want. However, it could help determine whether a local library is providing high-quality services for teens and the community,

Table 5.1. Plan for Change *(Columns Continued)*		
Leadership and Professionalism		
Below Basic	**Examples/Resources**	**Our Plan**
No line item for YA materials or staff.	YALSA White Paper: The Benefits of Including Dedicated Young Adult Librarians on Staff in the Public Library *Young Adults Deserve the Best: YALSA's Competencies in Action,* Chapter 1 "Defending the YA Budget," by Audra Caplan, *YALS*, Fall 2009	Examine budget, circulation, and staff statistics to determine whether levels are proportionate. Set as a goal in next year's budget to have at least one FTE YA librarian per branch; determine whether more are needed. Shift money from other areas to YA materials budget to achieve goal of proportionate materials.
Library staff, including the YA staff, are uninformed about Code of Ethics, Bill of Rights, Competencies, etc. YA staff do not read professional journals or belong to professional organizations.	*School Library Journal* *VOYA* *Journal of Research on Libraries & Young Adults* *YALS* YALSA issue paper: The Importance of a Whole Library Approach to Public Young Adult Library Services Institutional membership to YALSA Active involvement includes committee responsibilities, writing for professional journals, presentations at conferences.	Offer training to all staff on the YALSA Competencies. Work with all YA staff to include in their professional development plan that they are to be involved in a professional association. Allot one hour of off-desk time per week for professional association work. Subscribe to additional journals, and poll all staff to make sure journals are routed to all interested staff.

and that should be of interest to anyone who cares about the community. Anyone who is considering moving to a new community, especially if they have teenage children, or anyone who wants to become involved in the community, would find useful information by asking the library where they fit on this continuum. The place to start might be to ask questions of the teen services librarian and then to follow up about any areas of concern with the library's administration or trustees. It is also an opportunity to determine whether there are ways that library users and other community members could support the library in providing adequate resources and services for teens.

How Library and Information Science Faculty Can Use the Evaluation Tool

Library school faculty can use the tool in several different ways. First, the tool, along with the competencies that it is based on, can form the framework for a teen services curriculum, since all of the major elements of a good teen services program are included in the tool. The "Examples/Resources" column offers suggested readings that would be useful to students interested in learning more about specific areas.

Second, having students become familiar with the tool will help them identify the areas in which they can prepare themselves to become good teen services librarians. Looking at the "Access to Information" section, for example, could help a potential teen services librarian determine that he needed to learn some merchandising and marketing techniques to promote a YA collection, or that she needed to find some technology-related blogs to follow to keep up-to-date on advances that could improve teens' access to information.

Finally, faculty members could encourage students to use the tool to evaluate the libraries at which they may be considering job offers. Knowing that a library actively supports and promotes teen services and provides opportunities for its librarians to improve those services could be influential if a student has more than one job offer. On the other hand, in a tighter job market, where the opportunities are fewer, knowing that the library where one has just been hired rates as "Below Basic" on many items can provide a solid plan of attack for the ambitious teen services librarian. Even small changes forward on the continuum can make a big improvement in the overall service to teens and the community.

How Teen Services Librarians Can Use the Evaluation Tool

Teen services librarians can use the tool in many different ways and on many different levels. To start with, it can help a librarian determine whether there are areas that he or she can work on that will improve the library's service. It can serve as a basis for the librarian's professional development plan and help when setting goals with a supervisor. It can help the librarian identify areas of concern.

Many of the suggestions in this book for ways to evaluate a teen services program are aimed at the frontline teen services librarian. *Young Adults Deserve the Best: YALSA's Competencies in Action* (2011), my companion book to the competencies, is entirely aimed at frontline librarians, and the suggestions in that book are focused on helping the librarian achieve the competencies, which will, in turn, help the library reach the "Distinguished" level on the evaluation tool.

References

ALA (American Library Association). 2009. "Core Competences of Librarianship." American Library Association. http://www.ala.org/educationcareers/sites/ala.org.educationcareers/files/content/careers/corecomp/corecompetences/finalcorecompstat09.pdf.

Flowers, Sarah, for the Young Adult Library Services Association. 2011. *Young Adults Deserve the Best: YALSA's Competencies in Action.* Chicago: American Library Association.

YALSA (Young Adult Library Services Association). 2010. "YALSA's Competencies for Librarians Serving Youth: Young Adults Deserve the Best." American Library Association. http://www.ala.org/yalsa/guidelines/yacompetencies2010.

YALSA (Young Adult Library Services Association). 2011. "Public Library Evaluation Tool." American Library Association. http://www.ala.org/yalsa/guidelines/yacompetencies/evaltool.

6
References and Resource Guide

Links and Books

Following are some resources for doing evaluation in libraries.

- The Library Gaming Toolkit (http://librarygamingtoolkit.org/eval.html) contains information about evaluating a library gaming program and includes links to several surveys and evaluation tools from libraries that have done gaming programs. These could be adapted to other types of programs.
- The ALA Core Competences of Librarianship (http://www.ala.org/ala/education careers/careers/corecomp/corecompetences/finalcorecompstat09.pdf) list the areas in which graduates of accredited master's programs in library and information science should be knowledgeable.
- The American Association of School Librarians (AASL) Standards for Initial Preparation of School Librarians (http://www.ala.org/ala/mgrps/divs/aasl/aasl education/schoollibrary/2010_standards_with_rubrics_and_statements_1-31-11.pdf) apply to master's programs that prepare individuals to "develop and manage library and information services in a PreK–12 setting."
- AASL's *Empowering Learners: Guidelines for School Library Programs* (AASL, 2009) includes guiding principles for school library media programs.
- WebJunction's Competency Index for the Library Field (http://www.webjunction .org/c/document_library/get_file?folderId=67024497&name=DLFE-16500008.pdf) includes a section on Young Adult Services.
- *Guidelines for Library Services to Young Adults* by the International Federation of Library Associations and Institutions (IFLA, 2006) (http://archive.ifla.org/ VII/s10/pubs/ya-guidelines-en.pdf) includes a self-assessment checklist.
- For sample library employee evaluations, see the Library Research Service's website (http://www.lrs.org/documents/field_stats/Employee_Evaluations.pdf).
- For the basics on how to conduct a needs assessment, see the University of Arizona's Needs Assessment tutorial (http://intranet.library.arizona.edu/archives/ teams/nadm/tutorial/index.html).

- For more details about collecting data, see Virginia A. Walter's book, *Output Measures and More: Planning and Evaluating Public Library Services* (ALA Editions, 1995).
- For more about outcome measures, see Rhea Joyce Rubin's *Demonstrating Results: Using Outcome Measurement in Your Library* (ALA Editions, 2006) and Eliza Dresang's *Dynamic Youth Services through Outcome-Based Planning and Evaluation* (ALA Editions, 2006).

Sample Forms

Following are some samples of various kinds of evaluation tools. A note of caution: all surveys and evaluations should be customized to meet your particular needs. These are simply examples. As noted in Chapter 4, the type of evaluation you do will depend upon what your desired outcomes are: what kinds of decisions might be made as a result of your evaluation, who will see the results, and so on.

Needs Assessments

One of the keys to gauging success is knowing what your users expect and want. Doing regular needs assessments can help you keep up with what the teens in your community are thinking. Needs assessments should be done whenever the library is planning a new building or a major remodel, but they can also be done to check in on service needs and desires. A needs assessment can be comprehensive, or can focus on one small area, such as the summer reading program. Form 6.1 (pp. 75–76) is a general needs assessment that covers all aspects of the library's services: collections, programs, facilities, and hours.

There are various ways to use the information derived from a needs assessment like the one in Form 6.1. You could create a narrative report that sums up the highlights, for example, "Of those who did not regularly use the library, 80 percent said that they had no transportation or that the location was inconvenient, and 75 percent said the hours were not convenient." This is a good way to prioritize urgent concerns that were revealed in the survey. Or you could do a thorough analysis of all responses and create graphs or charts that show the numbers or percentages of respondents who, for example, had expressed a desire for more services of various types, as in Figure 6.1.

Summer Reading Programs

As mentioned in Chapter 4, there are many ways to evaluate a summer reading program, depending on your desired outcomes. Form 6.2 and Form 6.3 (pp. 76–77) are examples of pre- and post-evaluations for a summer reading program. Doing

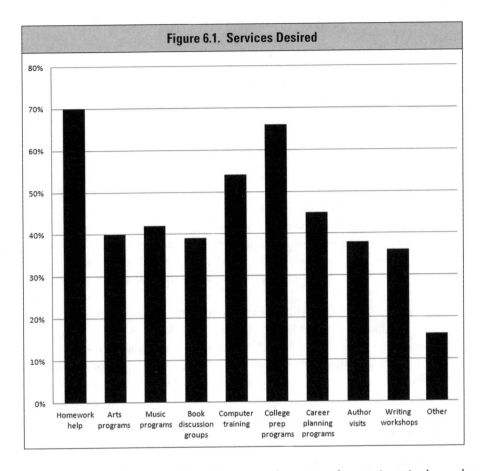

Figure 6.1. Services Desired

these types of evaluations will enable you to determine changes in attitudes and behaviors before and after participation in a summer reading program. This is the type of information you need for outcome-based evaluation. Form 6.4 (p. 77) is a simpler satisfaction survey that could be used in planning for future summer reading programs. It asks about user satisfaction with the programs and incentives offered and asks for suggestions for future summers.

Form 6.5 (p. 78) is based on the final report required for the New York State Library's 2011 Summer Reading mini-grant program, a project of the Library Services and Technology Act (LSTA) and the New York State Library's Division of Library Development. See http://www.nysl.nysed.gov/libdev/lsta/summer11/finalreport.doc for the full version. This would be the kind of evaluation form that you would share with supervisors and library administration. It covers all aspects of the program: participation, programs, publicity, and budget, and allows space for anecdotal reports. If you were doing outcome-based measures, those could also be included. This detailed information is also useful for planning in future years.

Form 6.6 (p. 79) is a simple summary report of the basic statistics from a summer reading program. It allows a quick glance at the success of the program, and is something that would be good to share with other library staff, by posting it on a bulletin board, or with the library board, as an insert into their agenda packet.

Program Evaluation

The types of surveys and forms from summer reading could also be used in regular program evaluation. Form 6.7 (p. 80) is an example of an evaluation form for a stand-alone library program. By using this form, the library is attempting to find out something about the teens who attended the program in order to plan for future programs. It includes questions about teens' access to the library and about how they learn about library programs. Form 6.8 (p. 81) is an even simpler survey to get immediate responses from teens who are attending a program. By keeping it short and sweet, they are likely to fill it out on the spot. It does not contain as much information, but it does give some instant feedback about the success of a program.

Form 6.9 (p. 82) is a reporting form, similar to the summer reading report in Form 6.5. This form is intended for reporting about the details of a program to library administration. It is also useful for the individual librarian to maintain information from program to program about what works, how costs vary, and how the program addressed both the library's mission and goals and the developmental needs of teens. Asking how teens were involved in planning or implementing the program is also a good reality check for teen services librarians, to remind them of the importance of teen involvement.

Staff Evaluation

Libraries have their own forms that are required for supervisors to evaluate staff. Form 6.10 (p. 83) is a survey form for members of the public to judge how well library staff have responded to their needs. It gives patrons an opportunity to express their satisfaction with the service provided by library staff. Both the advantage and disadvantage to this type of survey is that the respondents will answer the questions about the person they most recently, or most memorably, dealt with. This may or may not be a librarian, and it certainly may or may not be a teen services librarian. The advantage to this type of survey is that the overall results will give a picture of whether teens are being treated respectfully and adequately by all library staff. The disadvantage is that it may be impossible to know which staff members treated them well and which did not.

Form 6.11 (pp. 84–86) is a self-assessment form, based on the YALSA competencies, that the teen services librarian can use to determine areas in which he or she needs education and training.

Form 6.1. Sample Needs Assessment Survey

1. What is your age group?

❏ 11–12 ❏ 13–14 ❏ 15–16 ❏ 17–18

2. Do you have a computer at home? ❏ yes ❏ no

3. Do you have a smart phone (iPhone, Droid, etc.)? ❏ yes ❏ no

4. Have you used a public library in the past year? ❏ yes ❏ no

5. If yes, how often did you visit (check one)?

❏ Daily ❏ Several times a week ❏ Weekly
❏ Several times a month ❏ Monthly ❏ Several times a month
❏ Several times a year ❏ Once a year ❏ Other: _____

6. If you don't use a public library regularly, please tell us why (check all that apply):

❏ Not enough time ❏ Use my computer at home
❏ Doesn't have what I need ❏ No transportation/location inconvenient
❏ Hours are not convenient ❏ Don't know
❏ Use my school library ❏ Other: _____
❏ Buy my own books

7. How do you usually get to the library?

❏ Walk ❏ Drive myself ❏ Someone drives me
❏ Bike ❏ Bus/public transportation ❏ Other: _____

8. If you do use the library, what do you use it for (check all that apply)?

❏ Bestsellers/popular materials ❏ Sit and read
❏ Borrow books ❏ Meet friends
❏ Borrow audiobooks ❏ Do homework
❏ Borrow videos/DVDs ❏ Tutoring
❏ Borrow music CDs ❏ Get reference help from librarian
❏ Borrow electronic games ❏ Use library's computers/Internet
❏ Pick up materials on hold ❏ Get suggestions for reading
❏ Browse magazines ❏ Use library's electronic databases
❏ Attend programs/special events ❏ Other: _____

9. What materials should the library buy more of?

❏ Teen fiction ❏ Documentary DVDs ❏ Test prep materials
❏ Teen nonfiction ❏ Science fiction ❏ Career materials
❏ Teen audiobooks ❏ Fantasy ❏ Homework support
❏ Music CDs ❏ Mysteries ❏ Anime
❏ Feature film DVDs ❏ Magazines ❏ Graphic novels

10. What services would you like to see more of?

❏ Homework help ❏ Computer training ❏ Author visits
❏ Arts programs ❏ College prep programs ❏ Writing workshops
❏ Music programs ❏ Career planning programs ❏ Other: _____
❏ Book discussion groups

(Continued)

Form 6.1. Sample Needs Assessment Survey *(Continued)*

11. What qualities are most important to you in the library:

❏ Art exhibits   ❏ Homework center   ❏ Study carrels
❏ Browsing areas   ❏ Quiet study areas   ❏ Wireless access
❏ Café with refreshments   ❏ Places for individual study ❏ Listening stations
❏ Comfortable seating   ❏ Places for tutoring   ❏ Lots of computers
❏ Group study areas   ❏ Meeting rooms

12. What days are you most likely to use the library?

❏ Monday–Thursday   ❏ Friday   ❏ Saturday   ❏ Sunday

13. What times are you most likely to use the library?

❏ 7:00–9:00 a.m.   ❏ 9:00 a.m.–12 Noon   ❏ 12 Noon–4 p.m.
❏ 4:00–6:00 p.m.   ❏ 6:00–9:00 p.m.   ❏ After 9 p.m.

14. Do you access the library's website from home?   ❏ yes   ❏ no

15. When looking for library materials or information, which do you depend on most?

❏ Using the library online via its website
❏ Calling the library
❏ Going to the library to get help from staff
❏ Going to the library to look for materials or information on your own

---

Form 6.2. Summer Reading Program Pre-Survey

Age: _____   Grade: _____

1. Do you like to read?

❏ Yes   ❏ No   ❏ Don't know

2. What do you usually read for fun?

❏ Magazines   ❏ Nonfiction books (history, biography, science,
❏ Fiction books (science fiction,   self-help, true crime, music, hobbies, other)
   fantasy, realistic fiction,   ❏ Websites
   school stories, mysteries, series, ❏ Nothing
   horror, TV/movie spin-offs)   ❏ Other: _____

3. How much do you usually read for fun during a normal school week?

❏ One book   ❏ More than one book   ❏ A few blogs or websites
❏ Less than one book   ❏ A few magazine articles ❏ Nothing

4. Do you and your friends like to share books or talk about the books you read?

❏ Yes   ❏ No   ❏ Don't know

5. How well do you feel that you understand what you read?

❏ Completely   ❏ A little   ❏ Don't know
❏ Mostly   ❏ Not much

Form 6.3. **Summer Reading Program Post-Survey**

Age: _____   Grade: _____

1. Do you like to read?

   ❑ Yes   ❑ No   ❑ Don't know

2. What was your summer reading goal? _____ pages _____ minutes _____ books

3. Did you meet your goal?

   ❑ Yes   ❑ No   ❑ Don't know

4. If not, why not?

5. What was the best book you read this summer?

6. Did you talk with anyone about the books you read this summer?

   ❑ Yes   ❑ No   ❑ Don't know

7. How well do you feel that you understand what you read this summer?

   ❑ Completely   ❑ A little   ❑ Don't know
   ❑ Mostly   ❑ Not much

Form 6.4. **Summer Reading Program Evaluation**

Age: _____   Grade: _____

Summer reading goal: _____ pages _____ minutes _____ books

Actual summer reading: _____ pages _____ minutes _____ books

What was the best book you read this summer?

Did you attend any of the summer programs?   ❑ Yes   ❑ No

For each event you attended, rate it on a scale from 1 (awful) to 5 (awesome):

Guitar Hero Tournament	1	2	3	4	5
Candymaking	1	2	3	4	5
Film Festival	1	2	3	4	5
Street Art Program	1	2	3	4	5
End of Summer Awards Party	1	2	3	4	5

Did you like the incentives/awards?   ❑ Yes   ❑ No

What kinds of incentives/awards would you like for next year?

What kinds of programs would you like for next year?

Comments:

Form 6.5. Sample Summer Reading Program Final Report

Narrative Report

On a separate sheet:
1. Describe the program's purpose.
2. Describe the program's activities.
3. Describe any activities that were built into your program that illustrated reading with understanding and pleasure, e.g., teens writing reviews, book discussions, reading-related activities, etc.
4. Anecdotal Info: Please provide a minimum of two anecdotes about how this library program affected people who received the services.
5. Budget Info: Please explain, in detail, program expenditures.

Quantitative Report

A. Themes, Registration, and Completion

Please answer each question or type N/A where a question does not apply.
1. Library: _____
2. Contact name: _____
3. TOTAL number of teens who registered for the summer reading program: _____

B. Reading Totals

For participants recording by time read:
1. TOTAL number of teens who recorded by minutes read: _____
2. TOTAL minutes read by these teens: _____

For participants recording by books read:
3. TOTAL number of teens who recorded by books read: _____
4. TOTAL number of books read by these teens: _____

C. Programs

A program is defined as one planned session conducted by a staff member, outside performer, or other programmer—it does not include informal visits to the library to report on reading, etc.
1. How many total programs did the library offer for teens this summer? (Include programs related and unrelated to the Summer Reading Program theme.) _____
2. Total attendance at the teen programs? _____

D. Promotion

1. How did you promote the Summer Reading Program?

   a. TV _____
   b. Local Radio _____
   c. Local Newspapers _____
   d. Local Organization _____
   e. Local Business _____
   f. Library's Website _____
   g. School Visits _____ (how many: _____)
   h. Other: _____
      Describe: _____
      _____

E. Components

1. Reading lists, brochures, bookmarks, posters, or other printed materials, including publicity materials.

   a. Number of different materials created: _____
      Please specify type: _____
      _____
   b. Total number of copies of all materials printed: _____

Form 6.6. Summer Reading Program
Summary Statistics

HOURS READ	# OF TEENS
15 hours	
30 hours	
45 hours	
60 hours	
75 hours	
90 hours	
105 hours	
120 hours	
135 hours	
150 + hours	
TOTAL teens	
TOTAL hours	

_____ teen volunteers served a total of _____ hours

_____ teens attended a total of _____ events

_____ of teens at the _____ program
were first-time library visitors

Form 6.7. Sample Program Evaluation

1. Do you have a library card?
   - ❏ Yes
   - ❏ No

2. How often do you come to the library?
   - ❏ 3 times a week or more
   - ❏ Once or twice a week
   - ❏ A few times a month
   - ❏ A few times a year
   - ❏ This is my first visit

3. Is this your first time at a library program?
   - ❏ Yes
   - ❏ No

4. Who did you come with?
   - ❏ Parent(s)
   - ❏ Friends(s)
   - ❏ Sister(s) or brother(s)
   - ❏ Other family member(s)
   - ❏ Alone

5. How did you hear about today's program?
   - ❏ At the library
   - ❏ At school
   - ❏ From a friend or relative
   - ❏ From a poster outside the library
   - ❏ Library's Facebook page
   - ❏ Twitter
   - ❏ E-mail
   - ❏ Newspaper
   - ❏ TV or radio
   - ❏ Other
   - ❏ Library website

6. What is the best time for you to come to a library program?
   - ❏ Weekday afternoons
   - ❏ Weekday evenings
   - ❏ Saturday mornings
   - ❏ Saturday afternoons
   - ❏ Sunday afternoons

7. What was your favorite part about today's program?

8. What kinds of programs would you come to at the library?

9. What did you think of today's program?
   - ❏ Excellent
   - ❏ Good
   - ❏ Okay
   - ❏ Poor
   - ❏ Terrible

10. How likely are you to come back to the library for another program?
    - ❏ Very likely
    - ❏ Somewhat likely
    - ❏ Not at all likely
    - ❏ I don't know

11. How likely are you to come back to the library for other reasons?
    - ❏ Very likely
    - ❏ Somewhat likely
    - ❏ Not at all likely
    - ❏ I don't know

Age: _____   Grade: _____

Form 6.8. Program Evaluation Form

We want to hear from you!

**Rate today's program on a scale of 1 to 5,
where 1 = Awful and 5 = Awesome.**

****

Guitar Hero Tournament   1   2   3   4   5

What was good about it?

What would have made it better?

****

Form 6.9. Programming Worksheet

Name of staff person:

Date:

Program Theme or Purpose:

Date(s) and Time:

Length of Program:

Location(s):

One-Time Event/Ongoing Program:

PROGRAM COSTS

ELEMENT	DESCRIPTION	COST
Staff Time	Estimate hours spent	
Performer(s) Fee	Actual cost	$
Cost of Materials and Supplies	Refreshments, craft supplies, publicity materials, etc.	$
Donated Materials and Supplies	Estimate dollar value	$
Total Monetary Cost	Exclude staff and donated materials in total	$

EVALUATION

How did the program foster the library's mission statement and current strategic plan?

How did the program address the developmental needs of teens?

How were teens involved in planning/implementing the program?

Could the program be improved or changed?

Could the publicity have been done differently?

Was the performer:

❏ well-received ❏ on time ❏ able to engage the
❏ prepared ❏ skilled audience

What was the general audience response?

❏ enthusiastic ❏ participatory ❏ disengaged

Number of people attending event:

Did the expected audience attend?

Attach Relevant Flyers and Evaluation Forms

Form 6.10. Patron Satisfaction Survey

Please think about a recent visit (online or in person) or call to the library and respond to the following statements:

The help I received from library staff was:

❏ Very poor   ❏ About average

❏ Somewhat unsatisfactory   ❏ Superior

❏ Very satisfactory

I was treated well by the library staff member who helped me:

❏ Strongly disagree   ❏ Somewhat agree

❏ Somewhat disagree   ❏ Strongly agree

❏ Neither agree nor disagree

The library staff member who helped me (check all that apply):

❏ Was patient   ❏ Was impatient

❏ Was enthusiastic   ❏ Acted bored

❏ Listened carefully   ❏ Was unfriendly

❏ Was friendly   ❏ Didn't listen carefully

❏ Was responsive   ❏ Ignored me

The library staff member who helped me (check all that apply):

❏ Kept me waiting while she or he talked to someone else   ❏ Gave unclear answers

❏ Didn't understand what I wanted   ❏ Gave me the wrong information

❏ Had to ask others for help   ❏ Was very knowledgeable

❏ Spoke too slowly   ❏ Gave me exactly the information I needed

❏ Spoke too fast   ❏ Asked me to clarify what I wanted

❏ Was disorganized   ❏ Checked to make sure I had what I needed

   ❏ Checked to make sure I understood

In general, I am pleased with the way I am treated at the library:

❏ Strongly disagree   ❏ Somewhat agree

❏ Somewhat disagree   ❏ Strongly agree

❏ Neither agree nor disagree

Comments:

Form 6.11. Self-Assessment

This self-assessment is largely based on "YALSA's Competencies for Librarians Serving Youth: Young Adults Deserve the Best." It is intended to be used by an individual librarian to identify areas in which growth or learning are needed as he or she strives to provide the best possible library service to teens. After the survey is completed, the results can be used to identify a few areas on which to focus in creating a training and professional development plan for the year.

Leadership and Professionalism	Yes	Somewhat	No
I am familiar with the ALA Bill of Rights.			
I am familiar with the ALA Code of Ethics.			
I am familiar with the Interpretations of the Library Bill of Rights that deal with services for teens.			
I am a member of at least one professional association.			
I have a professional development plan.			
I know the principles and best practices of youth participation.			
I know how to attract, mentor, and train other staff about working with teens.			
Knowledge of Client Group	**Yes**	**Somewhat**	**No**
I am familiar with the developmental needs of teens.			
I keep up-to-date with popular culture of interest to teens.			
I keep up-to-date with technological advances of interest to teens.			
I understand and respect diverse cultural, religious, and ethnic values.			
I know how to identify and meet the needs of teens with special needs.			
Communication, Marketing, and Outreach	**Yes**	**Somewhat**	**No**
I have appropriate professional relationships with teens.			
I have developed relationships and partnerships with library staff and administrators and other youth-serving professionals in the community.			
I know how to advocate for teens and promote the role of the library in serving teens.			
I have a marketing plan for promoting teen services in the library, schools, and the community at large.			

(Continued)

Form 6.11. Self-Assessment *(Continued)*			
Communication, Marketing, and Outreach *(Continued)*	**Yes**	**Somewhat**	**No**
I understand and can explain the relationship between teen services and the library's core goals and mission.			
All staff in my library serve teens with courtesy and respect.			
All staff in my library know how to promote programs and services for teens.			
I know how to identify teen groups that are not yet served or underserved by the library.			
I know how to promote teen services directly to teens and through their parents, educators, and other youth-serving community partners.			
Administration	**Yes**	**Somewhat**	**No**
I have a strategic plan for library service with teens, based on their unique needs.			
I have designed and conducted a community analysis and needs assessment for teen services.			
I involve teens in planning and decision making in the library.			
I can develop, justify, administer, and evaluate a budget for teen services.			
I know the principles of creating physical facilities that meet teen needs.			
I have developed written policies that mandate the rights of teens to equitable library service.			
I know how to identify and defend resources (staff, materials, facilities, funding) that will improve library service to teens.			
I maintain documentation about teen programs and activities.			
I plan programs and services that utilize the skills, talents, and resources of teens.			
Knowledge of Materials	**Yes**	**Somewhat**	**No**
I can develop an appropriate collection of materials that meets the informational and recreational needs of all types of teens, including readers and nonreaders.			
I have a collection development policy that supports and reflects the needs and interests of teens.			

(Continued)

Form 6.11. Self-Assessment *(Continued)*

Knowledge of Materials *(Continued)*	Yes	Somewhat	No
I am familiar with a wide variety of literature for teens in traditional and emerging formats.			
I am familiar with a broad range of selection sources.			
I serve as a knowledgeable resource on teen literature for teens, parents, caregivers, and the community.			
Access to Information	**Yes**	**Somewhat**	**No**
I know how to organize physical and virtual collections in a way that maximizes easy, equitable, and independent access to information by teens.			
I use current merchandising and promotional techniques to attract and invite teens to use the collection.			
I provide access to specialized information such as community resources.			
I provide and promote information resources appropriate to both curriculum and leisure needs of teens.			
I know how to instruct teens in basic research skills, including how to find, evaluate, and use information effectively.			
I am familiar with technological advances and keep up with how they can improve access to information for teens.			
Services	**Yes**	**Somewhat**	**No**
I know how to design, implement, and evaluate programs that meet the developmental needs of teens.			
I can identify and plan services with teens in nontraditional settings (detention facilities, alternative schools, homeschool settings, hospitals, etc.).			
I provide accurate, nonjudgmental reference services to teens.			
I am flexible, friendly, positive, and unbiased in dealing with teens.			
I respect the privacy of teens in serving their reference and readers' advisory needs.			
I take the opinions of teens seriously, and ask for their input in developing collections, programs, and services.			
Totals			

Checklists

Form 6.12 (below) is a basic checklist for teen collections. It is included to encourage librarians to think about the kinds of materials they offer. Some libraries will include some of these items in other parts of the collection—adult nonfiction, for example—but these are all items that teens want and use, and the checklist will help you think about whether the teens in your library can find all of these items. The actual list of types of materials will change over time, as new formats and materials become available. The list is only a guideline, so feel free to modify it.

Form 6.13 (p. 88) is a checklist to help you look at your library's policies and procedures and how they relate to teens. A strategic plan that does not specifically mention teens is not necessarily a bad strategic plan, but the teen services librarian will want to look at it and see how teens might fit into the library's goals and strategies. In Chapter 4 we looked at ways to change the library's policies and procedures if you determine that they are inequitable to teens.

Form 6.14 (p. 88) is a budget checklist, or really more of a budget information form. Finding out these numbers may require some digging, but they can give you a picture of the library's spending priorities, and they will help you manage spending in the teen services area.

Form 6.15 (p. 89) is a facilities checklist. It will help you look at your library's overall space and analyze how the teen space fits into it.

Form 6.12. Collection Checklist

Does the library have a separate collection development policy for teen collections?

❏ Yes   ❏ No

Does the teen collection include:

- ❏ Hardcover fiction
- ❏ Hardcover nonfiction
- ❏ Paperback fiction
- ❏ Paperback nonfiction
- ❏ Series fiction
- ❏ Science fiction
- ❏ Fantasy
- ❏ Romance
- ❏ Horror
- ❏ Graphic novels
- ❏ Comic books
- ❏ Classics
- ❏ Materials in other languages
- ❏ Audiobooks
  - ❏ On CD
  - ❏ On stand-alone devices (e.g., Playaway)
  - ❏ Downloadable
- ❏ Popular music
  - ❏ On CD
  - ❏ Downloadable
- ❏ Films
  - ❏ Feature film DVDs
  - ❏ Non–feature film (e.g., documentary) DVDs
  - ❏ Downloadable video
  - ❏ Anime
- ❏ Console games
- ❏ Magazines
- ❏ Databases that support the curriculum
- ❏ Databases with information on popular culture topics

Are teens included in the collection development process?

❏ Yes   ❏ No

Form 6.13. Policies/Procedures Checklist

❑ Does the library have a strategic plan?
❑ Does the library have a set of core values?
❑ Does the library have a set of strategic goals and objectives?
    ❑ Do any of these specifically mention teens?
❑ Is there a separate mission statement for teen services?
❑ Is there a separate strategic plan for teen services?
❑ Are there specific strategic goals and objectives for teen services?

❑ Does the library have policies that are applied only to teen patrons?
❑ Does the library require parental permission for teens to use certain parts of the collection?
❑ Do the library's privacy policies apply to teens?
❑ Does the library have separate rules for computer or Internet use for teens?
❑ Are the library's circulation policies different for teens than for adults?
❑ Is formal government identification required to obtain a library card?
❑ Is a parental signature required for a minor to obtain a library card?
❑ Does the library's behavior policy treat teens equitably?

❑ Are there policies that can be changed to be more equitable to teens? List here:

❑ Does the library need new policies that specifically relate to service to teens? List here:

Form 6.14. Budget Checklist

Library's total operating budget: _____   Library's teen materials budget: _____
Library's total materials budget: _____   Library's adult materials budget: _____
Library's total personnel budget: _____   Library's children's materials budget: _____
Library's training/continuing education budget: _____

Which budget are the following materials allocated to:
Teen hardcover fiction: _____
Teen paperback fiction: _____
Hardcover nonfiction (curriculum support): _____
Paperback nonfiction (curriculum support): _____
Nonfiction (life issues and personal growth): _____
Graphic novels: _____
Console games: _____
Magazines: _____
Anime: _____
Feature film DVDs of interest to teens: _____
Non–feature film DVDs of interest to teens: _____
Teen e-books: _____
Teen audiobooks on CD: _____   on mp3: _____   Downloadable: _____
Popular music on CD: _____   Downloadable: _____

Form 6.15. Facilities Checklist

❏ Does the library have a separate teen area?

    ❏ Is the teen area clearly marked?

    ❏ Are adults or children allowed to use the teen area?

    ❏ Does the area include comfortable seating (e.g., lounge chairs, sofas)?

    ❏ Is the area clean?

    ❏ Is the area well-lit?

    ❏ Is the area in a location that allows for conversation without disturbing other patrons?

    ❏ Does the area include space for group study?

    ❏ Does the area include space for displays?

    ❏ Does the area include computers with Internet access?

    ❏ Does the area include listening stations?

❏ Does the library have wireless Internet access?

❏ Does the library have adequate outlets for laptops and other electronic devices?

❏ Is the library open evenings and weekends?

****

Total square footage of building:

Square footage of area designated for teens:

Square footage of area designated for children:

Shelving (by square footage or by shelving units) in teen area:

Total seats in building (lounge seating, seats at computers, seats at desks, tables, carrels):

Seats in teen area:

YALSA's Competencies and Evaluation Tool

As explained in Chapter 5, "YALSA's Competencies for Librarians Serving Youth" and the "Public Library Evaluation Tool" cover all of the basics of teen library programs and services. These two documents are included here for your convenience and are also available on YALSA's website at http://www.ala.org/yalsa/guidelines/yacompetencies 2010 and http://www.ala.org/yalsa/guidelines/yacompetencies/evaltool, where the competencies are available in Spanish as well.

YALSA's Competencies for Librarians Serving Youth: Young Adults Deserve the Best

---

YALSA's Competencies for Librarians Serving Youth: Young Adults Deserve the Best
Updated January 2010

Introduction

The Young Adult Library Services Association (YALSA), a division of the American Library Association (ALA) that supports library services to teens, developed these competencies for librarians who serve young adults. Individuals who demonstrate the knowledge and skills laid out in this document will be able to provide quality library service for and with teenagers. Institutions seeking to improve their overall service capacity and increase public value to their community are encouraged to adopt these competencies.

YALSA first developed these competencies in 1981, which were revised in 1998, 2003, and 2010. The competencies can be used as a tool to evaluate and improve service, a foundation for library school curriculum, a framework for staff training and a set of guiding principles for use when speaking out for the importance of services to teens in libraries.

Audiences for the competencies include:

- Library educators
- School and library administrators
- Graduate students
- Young adult specialists
- School librarians
- Library training coordinators
- Public library generalists
- Human resources directors
- Nonlibrary youth advocates and service providers

Area I. Leadership and Professionalism

The librarian will be able to:

1. Develop and demonstrate leadership skills in identifying the unique needs of young adults and advocating for service excellence, including equitable funding and staffing levels relative to those provided for adults and children.
2. Develop and demonstrate a commitment to professionalism and ethical behavior.
3. Plan for personal and professional growth and career development.
4. Encourage young adults to become lifelong library users by helping them to discover what libraries offer, how to use library resources, and how libraries can assist them in actualizing their overall growth and development.

(Continued)

YALSA's Competencies for Librarians Serving Youth:
Young Adults Deserve the Best *(Continued)*

Area I. Leadership and Professionalism *(Continued)*

5. Develop and supervise formal youth participation, such as teen advisory groups, recruitment of teen volunteers, and opportunities for employment.
6. Model commitment to building assets in youth in order to develop healthy, successful young adults.
7. Implement mentoring methods to attract, develop, and train staff working with young adults.

Area II. Knowledge of Client Group
The librarian will be able to:

1. Become familiar with the developmental needs of young adults in order to provide the most appropriate resources and services.
2. Keep up-to-date with popular culture and technological advances that interest young adults.
3. Demonstrate an understanding of, and a respect for, diverse cultural, religious, and ethnic values.
4. Identify and meet the needs of patrons with special needs.

Area III. Communication, Marketing, and Outreach
The librarian will be able to:

1. Form appropriate professional relationships with young adults, providing them with the assets, inputs, and resiliency factors that they need to develop into caring, competent adults.
2. Develop relationships and partnerships with young adults, administrators, and other youth-serving professionals in the community by establishing regular communication and by taking advantage of opportunities to meet in person.
3. Be an advocate for young adults and effectively promote the role of the library in serving young adults, demonstrating that the provision of services to this group can help young adults build assets, achieve success, and in turn, create a stronger community.
4. Design, implement, and evaluate a strategic marketing plan for promoting young adult services in the library, schools, youth-serving agencies, and the community at large.
5. Demonstrate the capacity to articulate relationships between young adult services and the parent institution's core goals and mission.
6. Establish an environment in the library wherein all staff serve young adults with courtesy and respect, and all staff are encouraged to promote programs and services for young adults.
7. Identify young adult interests and groups underserved or not yet served by the library, including at-risk teens, those with disabilities, non–English speakers, etc., as well as those with special or niche interests.
8. Promote young adult library services directly to young adults through school visits, library tours, etc., and through engaging their parents, educators, and other youth-serving community partners.

Area IV. Administration
The librarian will be able to:

1. Develop a strategic plan for library service with young adults based on their unique needs.
2. Design and conduct a community analysis and needs assessment.
3. Apply research findings towards the development and improvement of young adult library services.
4. Design activities to involve young adults in planning and decision making.
5. Develop, justify, administer, and evaluate a budget for young adult services.

(Continued)

YALSA's Competencies for Librarians Serving Youth:
Young Adults Deserve the Best *(Continued)*

Area IV. Administration *(Continued)*

6. Develop physical facilities dedicated to the achievement of young adult service goals.
7. Develop written policies that mandate the rights of young adults to equitable library service.
8. Design, implement, and evaluate an ongoing program of professional development for all staff, to encourage and inspire continual excellence in service to young adults.
9. Identify and defend resources (staff, materials, facilities, funding) that will improve library service to young adults.
10. Document young adult programs and activities so as to contribute to institutional and professional memory.
11. Develop and manage services that utilize the skills, talents, and resources of young adults in the school or community.

Area V: Knowledge of Materials
The librarian will be able to:

1. Meet the informational and recreational needs of young adults through the development of an appropriate collection for all types of readers and nonreaders.
2. Develop a collection development policy that supports and reflect the needs and interests of young adults and is consistent with the parent institution's mission and policies.
3. Demonstrate a knowledge and appreciation of literature for and by young adults in traditional and emerging formats.
4. Develop a collection of materials from a broad range of selection sources, and for a variety of reading skill levels, that encompasses all appropriate formats, including, but not limited to, media that reflect varied and emerging technologies, and materials in languages other than English.
5. Serve as a knowledgeable resource to schools in the community as well as parents and caregivers on materials for young adults.

Area VI. Access to Information
The librarian will be able to:

1. Organize physical and virtual collections to maximize easy, equitable, and independent access to information by young adults.
2. Utilize current merchandising and promotional techniques to attract and invite young adults to use the collection.
3. Provide access to specialized information (i.e., community resources, work by local youth, etc.).
4. Formally and informally instruct young adults in basic research skills, including how to find, evaluate, and use information effectively.
5. Be an active partner in the development and implementation of technology and electronic resources to ensure young adults' access to knowledge and information.
6. Maintain awareness of ongoing technological advances and how they can improve access to information for young adults.

Area VII. Services
The librarian will be able to:

1. Design, implement, and evaluate programs and services within the framework of the library's strategic plan and based on the developmental needs of young adults and the public assets libraries represent, with young adult involvement whenever possible.

(Continued)

YALSA's Competencies for Librarians Serving Youth:
Young Adults Deserve the Best *(Continued)*

Area VII. Services *(Continued)*

2. Identify and plan services with young adults in nontraditional settings, such as hospitals, homeschool settings, alternative education, foster care programs, and detention facilities.

3. Provide a variety of informational and recreational services to meet the diverse needs and interests of young adults and to direct their own personal growth and development.

4. Continually identify trends and pop-culture interests of young people to inform and direct their recreational collection and programming needs.

5. Instruct young adults in basic information gathering, research skills and information literacy skills—including those necessary to evaluate and use electronic information sources—to develop lifelong learning habits.

6. Actively involve young adults in planning and implementing services and programs for their age group through advisory boards, task forces, and by less formal means (i.e., surveys, one-on-one discussion, focus groups, etc.).

7. Create an environment that embraces the flexible and changing nature of young adults' entertainment, technological, and informational needs.

YALSA Teen Services Evaluation Tool

YALSA Teen Services Evaluation Tool

This is a tool for evaluating a public library's overall level of success in providing services to teens, aged 12–18. Potential users of this tool include library administrators, library trustees, teen services librarians, and community members and job seekers hoping to assess a library's commitment to teen services. The tool is not intended to be an evaluation of an individual teen services librarian, but rather of an institution's program; however, of necessity some things will apply specifically to teen services staff. The areas for evaluation are derived primarily from *YALSA's Competencies for Librarians Serving Youth: Young Adults Deserve the Best* (YALSA, 2010). Not every element of the rubric will apply to every library situation, but the tool can serve as a place to begin the conversation about what constitutes excellent public library service for teens.

Young Adult Library Services Association
Adopted by the YALSA Board January 8, 2011

Note: The table columns span facing pages and are intended to be read across the two pages.

(Continued)

YALSA Teen Services Evaluation Tool		
Leadership and Professionalism		
Essential Element	**Distinguished**	**Proficient**
Equitable funding and staffing levels	Library maintains line items in the budget for YA materials and staff at levels proportionate to YA usage and circulation.	Line item for YA materials budget; at least one librarian FTE devoted to YA services for each branch.
Commitment to professionalism and ethical behavior	All library staff demonstrate extensive knowledge of ALA Code of Ethics, ALA Bill of Rights, YALSA Competencies and Guidelines for Service to Teens. The library defends YA services and the rights of teens to privacy and access. YA staff are actively involved in at least one professional organization on the national, regional, state, or local level. Subscriptions to appropriate professional journals are provided by library and accessible to all interested staff.	YA staff demonstrate knowledge of ALA Code of Ethics, ALA Bill of Rights, and YALSA Competencies and Guidelines for Service to Teens; defend YA services and the rights of teens to privacy and access. YA staff belong to a professional organization and read appropriate professional journals.
Plan for personal and professional growth and career development	Written professional development plan in place for the YA staff that is updated yearly. At least one professional development activity (course, conference, etc.) is completed each year. Library supports and pays for all professional development.	YA staff have a professional development plan and have regular opportunities for professional development, at least some of which are paid for by the library.
Develop and supervise formal youth participation	Library has ongoing teen advisory group, teen volunteers, and opportunities for teen employment.	Library has ongoing teen advisory group OR teen volunteers OR teen employees.
Implement methods to attract, develop, and train staff working with young adults	Library routinely includes information about YA services in all staff development activities, including regular staff meetings. Staff at all levels are encouraged to learn about working with teens.	Library occasionally includes information about YA services in staff development activities and staff meetings. YA staff are supported in professional development and encouraged to share their knowledge with other staff.

(Columns continued)

YALSA Teen Services Evaluation Tool *(Columns Continued)*		
Leadership and Professionalism		
Basic	**Below Basic**	**Examples/Resources**
Line item for YA materials budget. Some staff (professional or paraprofessional) devoted to YA services.	No line item for YA materials or staff.	YALSA White Paper: The Benefits of Including Dedicated Young Adult Librarians on Staff in the Public Library *Young Adults Deserve the Best: YALSA's Competencies in Action,* Chapter 1 "Defending the YA Budget," by Audra Caplan, *YALS,* Fall 2009
YA staff read appropriate professional journals.	Library staff, including the YA staff, are uninformed about Code of Ethics, Bill of Rights, Competencies, etc. YA staff do not read professional journals or belong to professional organizations.	*School Library Journal* *VOYA* *Journal of Research on Libraries & Young Adults* *YALS* YALSA issue paper : The Importance of a Whole Library Approach to Public Young Adult Library Services Institutional membership to YALSA Active involvement includes committee responsibilities, writing for professional journals, presentations at conferences.
YA staff have no professional development plan but do have occasional professional development opportunities.	YA staff have no professional development plan or opportunities for professional development.	YALSA Webinars University classes Workshops ALA Annual Conference State and regional association library conferences
Library uses teen advisors on an ad hoc basis.	No teen input to programs or services.	Ladder of Young People's Participation: freechild.org/ladder.htm
Library staff are aware minimally of YA services but are not encouraged or trained to work with young adults.	Library staff are not offered opportunities to learn more about young adults.	*YALS* is routed to entire staff. Library offers workshops or presenters specific to working with teens. YALSA Speaker Database

(Table continued)

YALSA Teen Services Evaluation Tool *(Continued)*		
Knowledge of Client Group		
Essential Element	**Distinguished**	**Proficient**
Familiarity with developmental needs	All staff members receive training in youth development and understand that every library employee serves youth. YA staff know adolescent development theory. Staff receive training to ensure they are familiar with the Search Institute's 40 Developmental Assets.	All staff understand that every library employee serves youth. YA staff know adolescent development theory and are familiar with Search Institute's 40 Developmental Assets.
Current knowledge of technology and popular culture	Library supports current knowledge in the areas of technology and popular culture through formal professional development as well as the time necessary to read print/online resources (blogs, websites, journals, etc.) and test out tools that teens may want and need to use. Library collects data on an annual basis from young adults through surveys, observations or focus groups as to their interests in technology and popular culture.	Library supports current knowledge in the areas of technology and popular culture for the YA staff through formal professional development and the time necessary to read online/print resources. Library collects data every several years from young adults.
Demonstrated respect for diversity	Library completes formal, annual community studies at a schedule appropriate to the rate of changes within the community. Library collection, programs, and strategic plan reflect the variety of cultures in the community and around the world. YA staff reflects diversity of the community.	Library conducts occasional formal community studies. Library collection, programs, and strategic plan reflect the variety of cultures in the community and around the world.
Special needs patron issues addressed	Library community studies thoroughly address the question of services to young adults with special needs. The library cooperates with organizations devoted to young adults and special needs clients to provide appropriate library services. Young adult library spaces are ADA compliant. Young adult strategic plan includes services needed for special needs patrons.	Library community studies incompletely address the question of services to young adults with special needs. The library strives to cooperate with organizations devoted to young adults and special needs clients to provide appropriate library services. Young adult library spaces are ADA compliant.
		(Columns continued)

YALSA Teen Services Evaluation Tool *(Columns Continued)*		
Knowledge of Client Group		
Basic	**Below Basic**	**Examples/Resources**
YA staff know adolescent development theory and are familiar with Search Institute's 40 Developmental Assets.	Library staff working with young adults possess no training in adolescent development.	YALSA e-courses YALSA institutes Search Institute's 40 Developmental Assets for Young Adults *Young Adults Deserve the Best: YALSA's Competencies in Action,* Chapter 2
YA staff are aware of print/online resources regarding technology and popular culture and attempt to keep current. YA staff participate in at least one professional development opportunity each year on these topics.	YA staff are unaware of print/online and professional development opportunities regarding technology and popular culture.	YALSA blogs Teen Tech Week and Teen Read Week resources Teen-oriented magazines Popular culture websites and blogs
Library conducts incomplete or informal community studies. Library collection, programs, and strategic plan only recognize the largest demographic populations in the community.	Library collection, programs, and strategic plan only recognize the largest demographic populations in the community.	Programs, services, materials in multiple languages Popular culture needs/desires of different ethnic cultures (e.g., telenovelas, Bollywood, magazines)
Library community studies partially or informally address the question of services to young adults with special needs. Young adult library spaces are ADA compliant.	Young adult library spaces are ADA compliant.	Americans with Disabilities Act homepage: www.ada.gov

(Table continued)

YALSA Teen Services Evaluation Tool *(Continued)*		
Communication, Marketing, and Outreach		
Essential Element	**Distinguished**	**Proficient**
Form appropriate professional relationships with young adults	Library supports a culture where all staff act as role models to young adults, following the guidelines of the Search Institute's 40 Developmental Assets: interacting in a caring, encouraging manner with young adults, modeling responsible behavior and providing clear rules and consequences.	Library supports a culture where YA staff act as role models to young adults, following the guidelines of the Search Institute's 40 Developmental Assets: interacting in a caring, encouraging manner with young adults, modeling responsible behavior and providing clear rules and consequences.
Develop relationships and partnerships with young adults, administrators, and other youth-serving professionals in the community	Library creates a culture in which all staff are encouraged to develop community partnerships and collaborate on programs and services and given work-time to attend meetings and work on collaborative projects with other community groups.	Library creates a culture in which YA staff are encouraged to develop community partnerships and collaborate on programs and services.
Advocate for young adults and effectively promote the role of the library in serving young adults	Library policies and public relations emphasize the importance of young adult services for both young adults and the community. All staff are encouraged to advocate for teens within the community.	YA staff encouraged to advocate internally and in public relations for the value of services to young adults for both the young adults and the community.
Design, implement, and evaluate a strategic marketing plan	Library has a marketing plan tailored to young adult services, including promotion within the library, schools, youth-serving agencies, in web-based venues used by teens, and the community at large.	Library references young adult services in their institution-wide marketing plan.
Establish an environment in the library wherein all staff serve young adults with courtesy and respect, and all staff are encouraged to promote programs and services for young adults	Library rules and behavior codes are enforced fairly without regard to age. Customer service training for staff includes component on serving young adults. Staff are aware of young adult programs and services and frequently recommend them to teens and talk about them in the community.	Library rules and behavior codes are enforced fairly without regard to age. Customer service training for staff includes component on serving young adults. Staff are aware of young adult programs and services but do not regularly recommend them to teens or the community.
		(Columns continued)

YALSA Teen Services Evaluation Tool *(Columns Continued)*		
Communication, Marketing, and Outreach		
Basic	**Below Basic**	**Examples/Resources**
YA staff act as role models to young adults.	YA staff interact positively with young adults.	Search Institute's 40 Developmental Assets
YA staff communicate occasionally with community partners.	YA staff do not have relationships with community partners.	*Young Adults Deserve the Best: YALSA's Competencies in Action,* Chapter 3
YA staff work to establish a culture of advocacy both internally and in public relations.	YA staff do not advocate for young adults either internally or in public relations.	YALSA's Speaking Up for Library Services to Teens: A Guide to Advocacy YALSA Advocacy Toolkit
Library markets young adult services on an ad hoc basis, without a unifying marketing plan.	Library does not market young adult services.	Ohio Library Council: Marketing the Library (http://www.olc.org/ marketing/index.html)
Library rules and behavior codes are not consistently enforced across demographics. Customer service training does not include a component on serving young adults. Staff rarely serve customers outside the age range they feel comfortable and/or are assigned to work with regularly.	Library rules and behavior codes are not enforced fairly across demographics. Staff are not trained on serving young adults and do not feel comfortable with or do not feel the need to provide young adult services.	Rules regarding noise, food, number of people at one table or computer
		(Table continued)

YALSA Teen Services Evaluation Tool *(Continued)*		
Communication, Marketing, and Outreach		
Essential Element	**Distinguished**	**Proficient**
Identify young adult interests and groups underserved or not yet served by the library	On a regular schedule and at least once a year, library combines informal inquiries with formal research methods to identify gaps in service and new and emerging trends. Young adults are involved in identification efforts.	Library identifies gaps in service along with new and emerging trends through occasional usage of information inquiries and/or formal research instruments.
Promote young adult library services directly to young adults	Library uses a variety of communication tools, both high-tech and low-tech, to reach young adults directly with regular updates on programs and services. The library web presence includes section devoted to young adult services. The library uses technologies currently used by teens. YA staff visit schools and community agencies virtually or face-to-face at least twice a year.	Library uses at least one communication tool in addition to a web presence and print flyers to provide regular updates on programs and services. YA staff visit schools and community agencies virtually or face-to-face at least once a year.
Administration		
Essential Element	**Distinguished**	**Proficient**
Develop a strategic plan for library service with YAs based on their unique needs	Library has created a YA mission statement or strategic plan with goals that connect to the overall institutional mission statement with input from YA staff that is subject to ongoing (at least annually), output-based evaluation.	Library mission statement addresses teen services. A separate YA mission statement or strategic plan is in development with input from YA staff.
Design and conduct a community analysis and needs assessment	Programs and services are offered on the basis of needs articulated in a written community analysis and needs assessment. Young adults are involved in development of needs assessment.	Library has a community analysis and needs assessment that includes some data on young adults.
Develop, justify, administer, and evaluate a budget for YA services	YA department has a budget proportionate to young adult usage and circulation. Annual reports show young adult circulation, usage, materials spending, etc. Funding sources are identified and available for additional services and programs.	YA department has adequate funding for materials, staff, technology, facilities. Spending is planned annually. Special projects can be funded through separate requests to administration or other funding sources.

(Columns continued)

YALSA Teen Services Evaluation Tool *(Columns Continued)*		
Communication, Marketing, and Outreach		
Basic	**Below Basic**	**Examples/Resources**
Library investigates gaps in service through informal inquiries.	Library does not use any methods, formal or informal, to identify gaps in service.	Focus groups Print or online surveys Community demographics research Crowdsourcing
Library uses the web presence and print flyers to provide information about programs and services. YA staff occasionally visit schools and community agencies face-to-face.	Library does not market directly to young adults.	Teen services mobile app Library Facebook/MySpace page Library Twitter feed
Administration		
Basic	**Below Basic**	**Examples/Resources**
Library mission statement and strategic plan do not specify teen goals or services.	Neither library nor YA department has a strategic plan. YA staff operate in isolation.	YA Strategic Plan with short-term and long-term goals YA Mission Statements as guide to serving young adults in the community *Young Adults Deserve the Best: YALSA's Competencies in Action,* Chapter 4
Community analysis and needs assessment is in development.	Neither library nor YA department has a current community analysis or needs assessment.	Community Analysis and Needs Assessment Document Circulation and population statistics
Young adult materials and staffing are funded as part of the overall library budget but not recorded or tracked separately.	Inadequate funding for YA materials, staff, and programs.	Funding for materials in multiple formats Funding for staff Funding for programs and additional services Funding for spaces

(Table continued)

YALSA Teen Services Evaluation Tool *(Continued)*		
Administration		
Essential Element	**Distinguished**	**Proficient**
Develop written policies that mandate the rights of YAs to equitable library service	All library policies and practices reflect a commitment to intellectual freedom and equitable access. Policies and procedures are examined annually and developed collaboratively and ensure that collections, resources, and services are available to all teens.	All library policies and practices reflect a commitment to intellectual freedom and equitable access. Policies and procedures are addressed on an ad hoc basis with the help of YA staff when requested.
Document YA programs and activities	Library maintains thorough documentation of all young adult programs and activities, including information on presenters, statistics, evaluations, notes about successes and failures. Reports with abundant data and statistics are shared at least quarterly and published widely within the library and the community.	YA department maintains statistics on young adult programs and services. Information is reported periodically, at least annually, to library administration.
Use the skills, talents, and resources of YAs in programs and services	Teens are involved at every level of planning and presenting young adult programs and services. Teens are encouraged to use their skills in creating and implementing programs and services, volunteering, and applying for employment in the library.	Teens are involved in some aspects of planning and presenting young adult programs and services.
Dedicated spaces for young adults	The library includes a dedicated space for young adults that is open and staffed all hours that the library is open. This space is equal or greater than the percentage of the full square feet of the library as the percentage of teens in the community. The young adult space has been planned and is updated regularly with the assistance of young adults. The young adult space includes at a minimum print fiction, print nonfiction, media, technology and devices, and comfortable seating.	The library includes a dedicated space for young adults. The young adult space has been planned and is updated regularly with the assistance of young adults. The young adult space includes at a minimum print fiction, print nonfiction, media, technology and devices, and comfortable seating.
		(Columns continued)

YALSA Teen Services Evaluation Tool *(Columns Continued)*		
Administration		
Basic	**Below Basic**	**Examples/Resources**
Most library policies and practices reflect a commitment to equitable access for teens. Policies are not reviewed.	Young adults are limited in access to certain materials, services, or areas.	Collection development policy Challenged materials policy Patron confidentiality policy and practice Internet access policy Absence of barriers to access
YA department provides a basic report annually to the library administration.	Little or no reporting with regard to young adult services and programs is required.	Annual report to administration and library board Articles for professional journals Output data
Teens are occasionally consulted when the library is developing young adult programs and services.	Teens are never or rarely consulted in the development of programs and services.	Teen Advisory Group One-time or short-term focus groups Online polls
The library includes a dedicated space for young adults.	There is a young adult collection located in the library.	YALSA White Paper: The Need for Teen Spaces in Public Libraries YA Spaces of Your Dreams (*VOYA* column) *Teen Spaces*, by Kimberly Bolan for YALSA (ALA Editions)

(Table continued)

YALSA Teen Services Evaluation Tool *(Continued)*		
Knowledge of Materials		
Essential Element	**Distinguished**	**Proficient**
Collection development policy	Library maintains a YA collection development policy that is consistent with the parent institution's mission statement and strategic plan, includes materials in a variety of formats including print and digital, is reviewed annually, and YA staff have significant input into this plan.	Library maintains a separate YA collection development policy that is reviewed biennially with some input from YA staff. Policy includes plans for collecting materials in a variety of formats, including print and digital.
Knowledge of YA literature and selection sources	YA staff show a deep knowledge of young adult literature by reading two or more YA books per month and participating in multiple literary professional activities; review for a journal, write a review blog, participate in a Mock Printz or other workshops each year. Library subscribes to multiple review sources which are shared with all interested staff.	YA staff show a good knowledge of young adult literature by reading 1–2 YA books per month and participating in one other professional activity. Library subscribes to at least two different review sources and shares them with YA staff.
Collection of materials in a variety of formats, reading levels, and languages	Young adult collection represents a wide variety of formats including print and digital. The entire collection is continually evaluated and weeded. Collection reflects languages other than English that reflect the library community. YA staff are familiar with all types of materials that teens consume in all types of formats.	Young adult collection consists of print books, periodicals, and at least two other formats. Collection reflects the languages spoken in the library community. All areas of the YA collection have been weeded in the past 1–2 years.
Serve as a resource, liaison, and partner with schools, parents, and caregivers	YA staff visit area schools virtually or face-to-face at least once a year and together they work to collaborate on programs and services to young adults. YA staff regularly attend school events to liaise with teachers and parents.	YA staff visit area schools virtually or face-to-face at least once a year. YA staff attend one or two events at the school each year.
		(Columns continued)

YALSA Teen Services Evaluation Tool *(Columns Continued)*		
Knowledge of Materials		
Basic	**Below Basic**	**Examples/Resources**
Library maintains a collection development policy but does not have a separate document for young adults.	Library does not have a formal collection development policy.	*Young Adults Deserve the Best: YALSA's Competencies in Action,* Chapter 5
YA staff read ten YA books or less a year. Library subscribes to at least two review sources.	YA librarian does not read YA literature and the library does not subscribe to a review source for YA literature.	*School Library Journal* *VOYA* *ALAN Review* *Booklist* YALSA selected lists and awards YALSA literature blog
YA collection consists of print books, periodicals and one other format. YA collection has been weeded in the past 2–3 years.	YA collection consists mainly of print books and periodicals. The collection is out-of-date and hasn't been weeded in 3 or more years.	Formats may include: print, audio, video, video games, e-books, graphic novels, periodicals, downloadable music, etc.
YA staff communicate with area schools to ensure they are aware of library services and programs.	YA staff have no relationship with area schools and/or PTAs.	Monthly newsletter to teachers and school librarians School events include: open houses, back-to-school nights, PTA meetings, science fairs.
		(Table continued)

YALSA Teen Services Evaluation Tool *(Continued)*		
Access to Information		
Essential Element	**Distinguished**	**Proficient**
Organize the collection for ease of access	Library organizes physical and virtual collections to maximize easy, equitable and independent access to information by all young adults. Library consistently, at least annually, reevaluates the organization scheme to make sure it is still relevant to young adults.	Library organizes physical and virtual collections to provide easy and independent access to information by young adults and evaluates the scheme every 2–3 years.
Merchandise and market the collection	Library uses up-to-date merchandising and promotional techniques, including displays, print marketing and online tools to attract young adults to use the collection. Library consistently evaluates the organization scheme to make sure it is still relevant to young adults.	Library uses merchandising and promotional techniques including displays and print marketing in the library to attract young adults to use the collection. Promotional materials are updated regularly.
Provide instruction in basic research skills	YA staff use a wide variety of print and online tools to teach how to find, evaluate, use and credit information effectively. YA staff teach these skills formally and take every opportunity to teach in one-on-one and group interactions, both face-to-face and virtually, and encourage lifelong learning habits.	YA staff take initiative to formally teach how to find, evaluate, and use information effectively, using a variety of print and online tools.
Develop and provide access to technology and electronic resources	YA staff work with others in the library, the community, and the profession to build and share new technology and digital resources and tools that ensure young adults' access to knowledge and information. YA staff implement and integrate digital tools in programs and services on a regular basis.	YA staff are aware of new technology and digital resources and adopt them when convenient.
Maintain awareness of ongoing technological advances	YA staff weekly use a wide variety of tools, books, magazines, newspapers, blogs and microblogs, and podcasts to remain aware of advances in technology that can improve access to information for young adults and act as advocates for the adoption of these advances in the library.	YA staff use some tools at least monthly to stay aware of advances in technology that can improve access to information and incorporate them into the library when already approved by library administration.

(Columns continued)

YALSA Teen Services Evaluation Tool *(Columns Continued)*		
Access to Information		
Basic	**Below Basic**	**Examples/Resources**
Library has organized physical and virtual collections but needs to reevaluate and update to accommodate new or growing collections.	Library has organized physical and virtual collections, but they are not easy to use and the library has not reevaluated the organization structure.	Using consistent labels and tags on both print and online collections to make transition between print and virtual collections as seamless as possible *Young Adults Deserve the Best: YALSA's Competencies in Action,* Chapter 6
Library uses promotional techniques like displays and print marketing in the library to promote the collection. These are not updated often.	Library does not merchandise or promote the collection.	Facebook fan pages Web-based pathfinders Book blogs
When requested, YA staff formally teach how to find, evaluate, and use information.	YA staff do not teach research skills and do not model basic research skills.	Screencasts and pathfinders to teach students basic research skills Virtual tools wherever appropriate to community (e.g., mobile device reference app) Group instruction Turning every reference interaction into a teaching moment
YA staff are aware of new technology and digital resources but are unable to use them in the library.	YA staff are unaware of new technology and digital resources that increase young adults' access to information.	YA staff contribute to online information collections or initiatives.
YA staff are aware of advances in technology when library incorporates these advances into a larger technological upgrade but do not seek information about these topics.	YA staff are unaware of advances in technology that can improve young adults' access to information and do not update technology regularly.	Reading technology-related blogs and Twitter feeds Subscribing to technology-related podcasts
		(Table continued)

YALSA Teen Services Evaluation Tool *(Continued)*		
Services		
Essential Element	**Distinguished**	**Proficient**
Evaluate programs and services	Library programs and services meet the goals of the library's strategic plan while also meeting the developmental needs of young adults. Programs and services always include young adult involvement, through planning and implementation or volunteering, whenever possible.	Library organizes physical and virtual collections to provide easy and independent access to information by young adults and evaluates the scheme every 2–3 years.
Develop and implement services to young adults outside the library	YA staff initiate and foster partnerships with organizations outside the library to provide services with young adults in nontraditional library settings.	YA staff work with organizations that approach the library to provide services to young adults in non-traditional library settings.
Provide services that meet the needs and interests of young adults	Library provides a variety of services, both informational and recreational, that meet the needs and interest of a majority of young adults in the community while still ensuring that these services also meet the goals of the library as a whole.	Library provides services, both recreational and informational, that meet the needs of a majority of young adults in the community.
Provide programs and services current with young adult interest and trends	YA staff use a variety of tools, professional journals, magazines, online articles, etc., to remain aware of trends and pop-culture interests of young adults and use this knowledge on an ongoing basis to create new and improve existing library services and the library collection.	YA staff use tools like professional journals and magazines to remain aware of trends and pop-culture interests of young adults and periodically use this knowledge to improve existing library services and the library collection.
Accept the changing nature of young adult needs	Library is aware of and is prepared to adapt quickly to the flexible and changing nature of young adults' entertainment, technological, and information needs.	Library is aware of the flexible and changing nature of young adults' entertainment, technological, and information needs but needs time to act on these changes.

(Columns continued)

YALSA Teen Services Evaluation Tool *(Columns Continued)*		
Services		
Basic	**Below Basic**	**Examples/Resources**
Library programs and services meet the goals of the library's strategic plan but do not take into consideration the developmental needs of young adults.	Library programs and services do not have any driving goals connected to strategic plan or the developmental needs of teens.	YALSA Youth Participation Handbook Search Institute's 40 Developmental Assets *Young Adults Deserve the Best: YALSA's Competencies in Action,* Chapter 7
YA staff are aware of community organizations that serve young adults but do not partner with them to offer services.	YA staff are unaware of community organizations that serve young adults and methods of offering services in nontraditional library settings.	Outreach opportunities may include: hospitals, homeschool settings, alternative education facilities, foster care programs and detention facilities.
Library provides services, both recreational and informational, that meet the needs of some young adults.	Library does not provide services that meet the needs and interests of young adults.	Homework help College/career help Programs that support teen popular culture interests (e.g., gaming, anime, fanfic, etc.) Readers' advisory lists and displays
YA staff do not seek out information about current trends and pop-culture interest of young adults but, when the knowledge is available, improve library services and collections.	YA staff are not aware of trends and pop-culture interest of young adults.	YA staff are aware that new TV show based on a teen series will be airing soon and so order extra copies of the series to meet the predicted demand.
Library is aware of the flexible and changing nature of young adults' entertainment, technological, and information needs but does not act on these changes.	Library is unaware of the needs of teens.	School assignments New formats

References

AASL (American Association of School Librarians). 2009. *Empowering Learners: Guidelines for School Library Programs*. Chicago: American Library Association.

YALSA (Young Adult Library Services Association). 2010. "YALSA's Competencies for Librarians Serving Youth: Young Adults Deserve the Best." American Library Association. http://www.ala.org/yalsa/guidelines/yacompetencies2010.

Index

About the Author and YALSA

Sarah Flowers has worked as a young adult librarian, a supervisor of adult and young adult services, the manager of a community library, and as the deputy county librarian for the Santa Clara County Library in California, where she learned the practical details of analyzing and evaluating library data. She was a member of the top 40 distinguished alumni of the San Jose State School of Library and Information Science, and was a member of the first class of *Library Journal*'s "Movers and Shakers." She is the author of four nonfiction books for young people and numerous articles and reviews for library journals, as well as the author of *Young Adults Deserve the Best: YALSA's Competencies in Action* (ALA Editions, 2011). She has been active in ALA and YALSA for many years, and is the 2011–2012 President of YALSA.

The **Young Adult Library Services Association (YALSA)** is the fourth-largest division of the American Library Association, with more than 5,400 members. YALSA's mission is to expand and strengthen library services for teens and young adults. Through its member-driven advocacy, research, and professional development initiatives, YALSA builds the capacity of libraries and librarians to engage, serve, and empower teens and young adults. YALSA's major initiatives include Teen Read Week™ and Teen Tech Week™. Known as the world leader in recommending books and media to those ages 12–18, YALSA each year gives out six literary awards, including the Printz Award, and chooses titles for seven book and media lists. For more information about YALSA, visit http://www.ala.org/yalsa or http://www.ala .org/yalsa/booklists.